Praise for *Going Digital*

M000306970

'Here is the essential guide to how managers should adapt their businesses to the digital revolution. Written by a journalist who was the driving force behind the shift from print to digital in the *Financial Times* newsroom, the book offers many examples of how to change mindsets and work practices – and keep employees on board.'

Lionel Barber, Editor of The Financial Times 2005–2020

'Digital transformation is a daunting challenge. This wise, expert and supremely practical guide is an invaluable aid to navigating the nitty gritty of pushing digital change into the heart of your organisation. If you need to know where lean stops and agile starts, and how to craft a vision that truly heralds change this is the book for you. Highly recommended.'

Prof. Dr Lucy Kueng, digital transformation expert; Senior Fellow, Reuters Institute, Oxford University

'This is an ideal guide for anyone working in an industry where change is the only constant. Drawing on the experiences and advice of those who've been there before, it takes the mystery out of transformation showing the way to success in a digital world.'

Liz Hannam, Head of News, ITV News Central

'*Going Digital* is an essential survival kit in our journey of a constantly changing environment, giving the reader the inside and real view from champions behind the scenes sharing their tips on how to drive change at companies. It will become your bedside book.'

Berta Merelles, Senior Director, BTS Global Consultancy

'This book frames and filters that bigger dataset helping to benchmark one's own experience with examples from peers who faced similar challenges. Its value lies there, providing an understanding on how they responded and what succeeded, helping to lay out your own tailored approaches to these relatable problems.

The book serves that practical purpose. It is a great read and I was pleased to find out how many of the experiences paralleled what I had also encountered these past 18 months. It felt immediately like a validation that my journey was not uncommon and that I could learn something of value to my aspirations through the anecdotes of others.'

James Murray, Co-founder
and Chief Engineer, Offworld.ai

GOING DIGITAL

Pearson

At Pearson, we believe in learning – all kinds of learning for all kinds of people. Whether it's at home, in the classroom or in the workplace, learning is the key to improving our life chances.

That's why we're working with leading authors to bring you the latest thinking and best practices, so you can get better at the things that are important to you. You can learn on the page or on the move, and with content that's always crafted to help you understand quickly and apply what you've learned.

If you want to upgrade your personal skills or accelerate your career, become a more effective leader or more powerful communicator, discover new opportunities or simply find more inspiration, we can help you make progress in your work and life.

Every day our work helps learning flourish, and wherever learning flourishes, so do people.

To learn more, please visit us at **www.pearson.com/uk**

The Financial Times

With a worldwide network of highly respected journalists, *The Financial Times* provides global business news, insightful opinion and expert analysis of business, finance and politics. With over 500 journalists reporting from 50 countries worldwide, our in-depth coverage of international news is objectively reported and analysed from an independent, global perspective.

To find out more, visit **www.ft.com**

Lyndsey Jones
Balvinder Singh Powar

GOING DIGITAL

WHAT IT TAKES FOR SMOOTHER TRANSFORMATIONS

Pearson

Harlow, England • London • New York • Boston • San Francisco • Toronto • Sydney
Dubai • Singapore • Hong Kong • Tokyo • Seoul • Taipei • New Delhi
Cape Town • São Paulo • Mexico City • Madrid • Amsterdam • Munich • Paris • Milan

PEARSON EDUCATION LIMITED
KAO Two
KAO Park
Harlow CM17 9NA
United Kingdom
Tel: +44 (0)1279 623623
Web: www.pearson.com/uk

First edition published 2022 (print and electronic)
© Pearson Education Limited 2022 (print and electronic)

ISBN: 978-1-29-237567-0 (print)
    978-1-292-37569-4 (PDF)
    978-1-292-37568-7 (ePub)

British Library Cataloguing-in-Publication Data
A catalogue record for the print edition is available from the British Library

Library of Congress Cataloging-in-Publication Data
A catalog record for the print edition is available from the Library of Congress

10 9 8 7 6 5 4 3 2 1
25 24 23 22 21

Cover design by Two Associates

Print edition typeset in 9.5/13, Helvetica Neue LT W1G by Straive
Printed by Ashford Colour Press Ltd, Gosport

NOTE THAT ANY PAGE CROSS REFERENCES REFER TO THE PRINT EDITION

From Lyndsey Jones

For David, my husband, sounding board and tactician

From Balvinder Singh Powar

For Satinder 'Sunny' Singh Powar, my identical twin; even though
you are far away, this book is a way to honour your inspiration, creativity
and memory

CONTENTS

Pearson's Commitment to Diversity, Equity and Inclusion

Pearson is dedicated to creating bias-free content that reflects the diversity, depth and breadth of all learners' lived experiences. We embrace the many dimensions of diversity including, but not limited to, race, ethnicity, gender, sex, sexual orientation, socioeconomic status, ability, age and religious or political beliefs.

Education is a powerful force for equity and change in our world. It has the potential to deliver opportunities that improve lives and enable economic mobility. As we work with authors to create content for every product and service, we acknowledge our responsibility to demonstrate inclusivity and incorporate diverse scholarship so that everyone can achieve their potential through learning. As the world's leading learning company, we have a duty to help drive change and live up to our purpose to help more people create a better life for themselves and to create a better world.

Our ambition is to purposefully contribute to a world where:

- Everyone has an equitable and lifelong opportunity to succeed through learning.
- Our educational products and services are inclusive and represent the rich diversity of learners.
- Our educational content accurately reflects the histories and lived experiences of the learners we serve.
- Our educational content prompts deeper discussions with students and motivates them to expand their own learning and worldview.

We are also committed to providing products that are fully accessible to all learners. As per Pearson's guidelines for accessible educational Web media, we test and retest the capabilities of our products against the highest standards for every release, following the WCAG guidelines in developing new products for copyright year 2022 and beyond. You can learn more about Pearson's commitment to accessibility at:

https://www.pearson.com/us/accessibility.html

ABOUT THE AUTHORS

Lyndsey Jones is the lead author who was inspired to write *Going Digital* after spending several years leading digital transformation projects at the *Financial Times*.

She is currently a consultant, strategic advisor and coach working with media companies across Africa and Europe on digital transformation of their newsrooms, from operations to content strategy. She is also an international speaker, guest lecturer and business mentor.

As an executive editor at the FT, she played a key role in streamlining editorial operations and reshaping the newsroom to shift its main focus and mindset from print to digital publishing and collaborating with colleagues, teams and the union to secure buy-in to change.

Lyndsey was the architect of the 'broadcast schedule' aligning content publication with peak audiences to boost traffic, engagement and subscription revenue. She also devised and implemented a content reduction strategy to allow resources to focus on delivering the FT's gold standard journalism in digital formats.

Balvinder Singh Powar is the co-author and an adjunct professor and business mentor at IE Business School in Madrid, specialising in leadership, team management and motivation, innovation culture, mediation and conflict resolution, and entrepreneurship globally.

He co-developed a system called 'Unfold Work' in 2019 on how to create effective virtual hybrid teams with a focus on 'distributed work', where group interaction, neuroscience and agile and lean methodologies are key.

He is also a founding partner, board member and director at Booster Space Industries and Aerdron, which are both new space/aerospace consultancies.

Balvinder is passionate about the importance of building strong and effective teams and enabling projects, which push boundaries. He is a strong advocate of self-empowerment and pro-activeness to achieve one's goals, with his favourite quote being that of Mahatma Gandhi: "Be the change you want to see in the world."

In 2015 he became a business mentor at The Founder Institute, one of the largest start-up networks. In 2017 he became a partner at B-Scaled, a consultancy helping mainly tech start-ups to find clients and investment globally. His current focus is on wellbeing projects in the therapy, mindfulness and hydroponic food production sectors.

English of Indian origin, and resident in Spain, he is a business and finance graduate who also studied a masters in mediation from the University of London. He has extensive experience leading business, social, cultural, media and technology projects in Spain and internationally.

AUTHORS' ACKNOWLEDGEMENTS

LYNDSEY JONES

I'd like to thank the following people for their inspiration, encouragement, buy-in and help in making this book happen.

At Pearson, commissioning editor Eloise Cook for believing in the kernel of my idea and then helping us craft it into a much better book. Her advice and comments were invaluable.

James Lamont, the then managing editor at the *Financial Times*, for encouraging me to pursue the idea, and Andrew Hill for initially helping to shape a proposal.

Every FT journalist who gave me a tip, contact or piece of advice, and in particular Harriet Arnold, Claer Barratt, Daniel Dombey and Christopher Grimes for putting me in touch with people I later interviewed.

And to all the interviewees who spared their time to talk to us candidly about what it took to make change happen.

FT columnist Brooke Masters and author Fran Abrams, both of whom warned me how long it was going to take to write a book (months) and that I had seriously underestimated it (weeks). They were right.

Tony Major, former assistant editor at the FT, who asked me to help lead and manage a digital transformation project, which involved not only changing the print production operation, but also working practices in the newsroom.

That experience led me to other transformation projects, where I became the architect of the *broadcast* schedule, a global online publication system, working alongside the then head of news, Peter Spiegel. And later, I devised a strategy to prioritise value over volume, reducing the number of stories published.

And to all the journalists that I have had to cajole, trick or laugh, and enforce (aka encourage, influence and persuade) into changing their working practices.

All of this change management experience inspired the idea for this book.

Balvinder Singh Powar for agreeing to come on this crazy journey with me at what turned out to be not only a crazy time for the world but for him personally. He pulled the stops out to give his insights and change management expertise for which I am deeply grateful.

My parents, Glenda and Alan Jones, for not only encouraging me to become a journalist in the first place but also listening every night for several months to my updates on the progress and process of writing this book.

And finally, my husband David Bell for all the advice he gave me when I was navigating digital transformation during my career, whose strategic nous and logic helped me to tackle the challenges that I faced at the time.

BALVINDER SINGH POWAR

First of all, I would like to thank Lyndsey for inviting me on this crazy journey. From an idea it has become a rollercoaster ride at the toughest period of my life, but has kept me going and challenged me to get out of my comfort zone. Her discipline, determination and writing skills have made it happen and on time.

To Eloise Cook who has generously guided us so that we could hone the book for the target audience.

My family – wife Estrella, kids Kiran and Kayla – who have supported me and given me space to work on something that was much tougher than I expected but also more rewarding than imagined. They have been at the coalface of my stress in completing the book.

My mum (Surinder Powar) and dad (Jagdish Powar) who always did their best and made education a key driver for our future success. My brothers Raja (Rajinder) and Sunny (Satinder) who inspired me to always better myself.

The interviewees, contributors, friends, family and supporters who encouraged us and shared their wisdom for the book.

All the people who have inspired me and helped me on my learning journey: professors, writers, colleagues, students, thought leaders, artists, entrepreneurs and risk takers.

IE University and Headspring, an FT/IE joint venture, for shaping the professor and trainer I am and giving me so many opportunities such as meeting Lyndsey in the first place.

PUBLISHER'S ACKNOWLEDGEMENTS

3 and 15 Mark Lillie: Quoted by Mark Lillie; **4 Strategyzer AG:** The Value Proposition Canvas by Strategyzer AG. Used by permission from Strategyzer AG. Retrieved from https://www.strategyzer.com/canvas/value-proposition-canvas/ ; **6, 10, 86–87 and 88 Saswati Saha Mitra:** Quoted by Saswati Saha Mitra; **6, 9, 11, 15, 59, 71, 73, 80, 94, 97, 127, 128, 129, and 130–131 Michelle Senecal de Fonseca:** Quoted by Michelle Senecal de Fonseca; **7 and 17 Thomas Stamm:** Quoted by Thomas Stamm; **9 Mithun Sridharan:** Mindmap: A tool for creativity & structured thinking, Mithun Sridharan January 24th, 2018 ; **11, 23, 89 and 90 Robert Shrimsley:** Quoted by Robert Shrimsley; **11, 20, 23, 24 and 34 Tom Fortin:** Quoted by Tom Fortin; **14, 21, 23, 80, 115 and 131 Anastasia Leng:** Quoted by Anastasia Leng; **15, 32, 52, 59, 93, 97, 128, 129 and 131 Michael Davison:** Quoted by Michael Davison; **16 and 79 Blathnaid Healy:** Quoted by Blathnaid Healy; **17, 47, 49, 52 and 58 Phil Neal:** Quoted by Phil Neal; **20, 21, 22 and 33 Marta Javaloys:** Quoted by Marta Javaloys; **25 Thomas Watson:** Quoted by Thomas Watson; **25 Jim Keyes:** Quoted by Jim Keyes; **25, 61–62, 71–72, 74 and 90 Abe Smith:** Quoted by Abe Smith; **26 Reena SenGupta:** Quoted by Reena SenGupta; **26-27, 42, 47, 73, 88 and 128 Anne Boden:** Quoted by Anne Boden; **28 Praxie, Inc.:** What is a Change Resistance Management Plan, and what are best practices, tools and online templates for teams and organizations?, https://praxie.com/change-resistance-management-plan-online-software-tools-templates-2-2/; **30 and 33 Sarah Wells:** Quoted by Sarah Wells; **30, 32, 46, 64–65, 78–79, 104–105, 123 and 131 Meri Williams:** Quoted by Meri Williams; **30, 73, 76, 88 and 98–99 Nico Arcauz:** Quoted by Nico Arcauz; **31, 70 and 75 Frank De Winne:** Quoted by Frank De Winne; **42 Amanda Murphy:** Quoted by Amanda Murphy; **43 Toyota:** World of Toyota this is Toyota the Toyota Way, https://www.toyota.com.cy/world-of-toyota/this-is-toyota/the-toyota-way; **43 Eric Ries:** Quoted by Eric Ries; **46 McKinsey & Company:** Lean management or agile? The right answer may be both, https://www.mckinsey.com/business-functions/operations/our-insights/lean-management-or-agile-the-right-answer-may-be-both; **46 Peter Drucker:** Quoted by Peter Drucker; **46 and 48–49 Fiona**

Spooner: Quoted by Fiona Spooner; **46 and 48 Robin Kwong:** Quoted by Robin Kwong; **53 Taihei Shigemori:** Quoted by Taihei Shigemori; **53 Daniel Hegarty:** Quoted by Daniel Hegarty 53–54, **55 and 125 Pablo Fernandez Iglesias:** Quoted by Pablo Fernandez Iglesias; **56, 113, 115 and 132 Nneile Nkholise:** Quoted by Nneile Nkholise; **57 and 60 Trond Sundnes:** Quoted by Trond Sundnes; **60 Satya Nadella:** Quoted by Satya Nadella; **61 Jennifer Tejada:** Quoted by Jennifer Tejada; **61, 89, 92, 124 and 126 Connie Nam:** Quoted by Connie Nam; **64 Daniel Goleman:** Quoted by Daniel Goleman; **65 Meredith Belbin:** Quoted by Meredith Belbin; **66–67 BELBIN Associates:** The Nine Belbin Team Roles, www.Belbin.com; **69 A H Maslow:** Based on Maslow's Maslow's Hierarchy of Needs; **70 Andy Pierce:** Quoted by Andy Pierce; **74 Harvard Business Publishing:** Adapted from "Begin and Trust," by Frances Frei and Anne Morriss, May-June 2020; **84 David Vivancos:** Quoted by David Vivancos; **84 The U.S. Chamber of Commerce Foundation:** From US Chamber of Commerce Foundation website; **85 Carly Fiorina:** Quoted by Carly Fiorina; **85 and 95 McKinley Hyden:** Quoted by McKinley Hyden; **85 and 96–97 Hogan Lovells:** Quoted by Hogan Lovells; **87 Thomas H. Davenport:** Quoted by Thomas H. Davenport; **88 and 95 Alberto Levy:** Quoted by Alberto Levy; **90, 91 and 112 Gustaf Nordbäck:** Quoted by Gustaf Nordbäck; **95 Timothy Holroyde:** Quoted by Lord Justice Holyroyde; **102, 103, 104, 110, 111, 114, 116 and 117 Priscilla Baffour:** Quoted by Priscilla Baffour; **102 and 107 Tom Ogletree:** Quoted by Tom Ogletree; **103, 104, 105, 107, 109, 112, 113, 114 and 117 Femi Otitoju:** Quoted by Femi Otitoju; **104 and 108–109 Liz Lowe:** Quoted by Liz Lowe; **107 and 116 Elyssa Byck:** Quoted by Elyssa Byck; **121, 124, 125 and 130 Elisabetta Galli:** Quoted by Elisabetta Galli; **121 Kanwarjit Singh:** Quoted by Kanwarjit Singh; **124, 125 and 127 Gerd Leonhard:** Quoted by Gerd Leonhard; **129 Nicholas Bloom:** Quoted by Nicholas Bloom.

FOREWORD

Santiago Iniguez
President IE University

"It was the best of times, it was the worst of times [. . .] it was the spring of hope, it was the winter of despair, we had everything before us, we had nothing before us . . . " These familiar lines are from the start of Charles Dickens' *A Tale of Two Cities*, one of the most celebrated literary openings ever written. They seem as opposite today as they were to the French Revolution – the context of the novel – and even to Dickens' times.

Supposedly, every century brings at least one revolution and we are, more or less perceptibly, living through ours: a major societal shift that has accelerated with the pandemic, along with other factors like the amazing developments in technologies, the changes in the profile and values of younger generations, along with the conflicting forces of globalisation and local diversity, which are all shaping a new model of society.

It is understandable that, caught in the middle of this maelstrom, many managers and entrepreneurs feel uneasy and anxious. At the same time, the current circumstances provide an arena where true leadership can be tested, and where managers can identify new opportunities or reinvent their existing businesses: it is time for the survival of the fittest, in Darwinian terms, or for the birth of new species that better adapt to this new environment.

The present book by Lyndsey Jones and Balvinder Singh Powar provides an excellent guide to navigate the challenging business environment. Both authors know business from the inside and have advised managers at companies from varied industries and territories. Their global experience in executive development is reflected in the fluid and didactic style of the book, with takeaways to be implemented in daily circumstances at work.

We live in times of access to more information than never before. Data has become an essential asset for strategic decision making, and *Going Digital* facilitates the tools to manage complexity competently.

Current exceptional circumstances demand all the skills associated with strong leadership: an entrepreneurial drive; the formulation of a future vision, despite uncertainties and alternative scenarios; motivating our people; determination and agile implementation of decisions, and most of all, resilience.

Resilience comes through character building, the repetition of behaviors and mental exercises. In many educational institutions, especially in military academies, this is drilled into students over a period of years. It is a quality that is useful for leaders in all fields, especially in business, and at times of extreme uncertainty such as today's. Entrepreneurs understand this all too well; after all they are serial losers: triumph only comes after repeated failure. Success is simply the other face of defeat.

However, times of crisis provide the breeding ground for entrepreneurs and innovators, and many major companies, some standing solidly today after decades, were created under adverse circumstances. To paraphrase Dickens, the worst of times often provides the best of times too.

We live in a brave new world where all business stakeholders face the challenge of transforming the world for the better. In this context, good business can be the best antidote to most of our global threats. Indeed, management can be one of the noblest professions and I hope that you find in this book valuable clues to fulfil this high mission.

CHAPTER 1

START AS YOU MEAN TO GO ON

Your business is likely to be going through continuous change as companies grapple with shifting consumer habits, new technologies and digital disruption. As a manager in this environment, you are likely to have to lead your team through digital transformation. You may need to transform one or more departments. Perhaps you have to change business operations or working practices at a legacy company. Or you may be trying to change customer behaviour to embrace digitalisation and boost revenue.

While you lead these types of projects, the path you take to delivering change is likely to be up to you and it can be daunting to know where to begin. Not only that, many of these types of projects fail and can come at a financial, reputational and human cost if you do not fully prepare.

One of the keys to success is having a robust plan to help you deliver change. Here we will not only show you how to draw one up, what you will need to do and when but also why it is important and how much preparation you will need to do beforehand to ensure you will succeed.

We spoke to close to 50 managers and founders from start-ups to multinationals, in a range of sectors including media, utilities, consumer goods, technology and financial services. They have shared their experiences and examples of best practice of what it is really like to lead and manage change and what it takes to make transformation happen.

WHY PLAN?

All the companies we spoke to took a systematic approach to planning, giving them a higher probability of success by thinking ahead, setting objectives and having a vision of what they would like to achieve. There are different versions of planning – some are meticulous, while others are fluid, evolving sequentially, especially in a fast-paced digital world.

By using data to back up your way forward, and making a clear roadmap, you will be giving yourself a greater chance of delivering the project than if you left things to chance.

A plan will help you sell your idea to your colleagues, aiding their understanding of why the project is necessary and what it means for the business – and possibly their roles. A visible timescale of tasks, of what is to be achieved by when, will help you see whether the project is on track or not. Expectations and resources can be adjusted accordingly.

Without a plan, you will not be able to review and you will not know whether you are on track.

IDENTIFY YOUR PROBLEM

Your first step should be to identify the problem from the customer's perspective and why solving it would add value to the business. This is a standard approach and one that all of the companies we spoke to took on a range of issues, placing the customer at the centre of their transformation.

Managers were typically attempting to work out what the problem was, such as CNN's London newsdesk devising and delivering a newsletter on the coronavirus pandemic, or the Spanish utility Iberdrola switching 11 million people to smart meters, in order to drive change.

This line of action was also adopted by the Google Search engineering team when thinking about how to tackle a huge drop-off rate in how people searched in global markets, as well as the Lawn Tennis Association (LTA), the British governing body, when planning to standardise how 6,000 coaches contact the business to make it more integrated and accessible.

"The mantra we have is: fall in love with the problem," says Mark Lillie, global technology strategy and transformation leader at Deloitte, a professional services company. He advises clients, including the LTA, on transformation projects. "Digital is ultimately about solving a problem, whether that is to make an audience's life simpler, or their experience more efficient, more impactful, more enjoyable."

Alberto Levy, international MBA professor and start-up mentor at IE Business School in Madrid, agrees: "Don't marry the solution, marry the problem. And once you marry the problem, you have got to find different solutions in a lot of organisations." This is because the issues in legacy businesses are unlikely to be solved by a product that was bought 'back in the day'.

But Mark Lillie warns that you must be clear about what the customer needs are as much as that broader line of becoming a digital business: "We did quite a lot of research around those current audience experiences and how we can use digital to make it better. That was quite a good exercise."

PAINT YOUR CANVAS

You can use a similar approach by doing a gap analysis that can help you to put the customer at the heart of transformation.

One tool that can help you to build on your gap analysis is the 'value proposition canvas' devised by Alexander Osterwalder and Yves Pigneur, who co-authored the book *Business Model Generation*. It shows you how you can work out your customer's problem and satisfy their needs – why they chose your company over another.

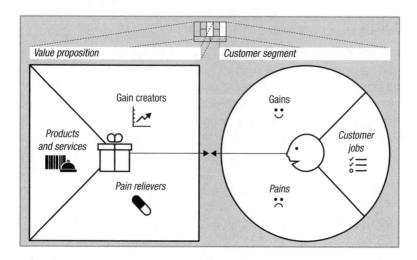

Figure 1.1 The value proposition canvas

The key to using the canvas is to make sure there is a match between the product and the market. We consistently heard from our interviewees that the innovation they proposed had to solve a problem for the client and meet their needs. If your project does not solve a real problem, what value can it bring? If it does not bring value, it will not be sustainable because customers will be unlikely to pay for it.

The canvas is a highly effective tool to collect data and create products and services deploying a visual guide that can make your planning more efficient and focused. You could also use a template to lay out what you need to include in your plan, spelling out the key elements, the time line and teams needed to help you.

EXERCISE

To use the value proposition canvas tool, you have to first enter into the mind and lifestyle of your target customer. You need to make assumptions which you can later test by interviewing potential clients. You need to have two rounds on the canvas:

- *Make assumptions*
- *Test those assumptions*

This gives you a deeper and more realistic understanding of your customers' social, functional and emotional needs.

Fill in the canvas template following these four steps:

1 Choose your target customer or segment.

2 Identify the jobs (tasks, problems, wishes) and prioritise them according to customer importance.

3 Identify and prioritise the gains or benefits.

4 Identify and prioritise the pains or negative experiences.

Once you have completed this, you can start to make a plan with a customer value focus.

FILL IN THE GAPS

Think about where you are now and where you want to go. If the best result is a 10, what level are you at now? Are you at 3 where the conversations have started and you are beginning to create a vision? So, what do you need to do to go from 3 to 10?

At Iberdrola, for example, part of its planning process was working out what its goal was going to be and what technology it needed to create to deliver the project.

Consider what you would like to achieve and understand how to get there, as well as weighing up whether you will need help.

Ask yourself questions such as these in the table to fill in the gap, frame the challenge and quantify the elements you need to achieve your 10.

	Current state	Desired state	Gaps	Solutions	Rating 1–10
Is there demand for this?					
Can you, your team or company do it?					
Is it worth it?					
Where do you want to be by a certain date?					
What does success look like?					

▶

	Current state	Desired state	Gaps	Solutions	Rating 1–10
How do you measure progress?					
What is the smallest step you need to take?					
Will you have enough resources?					
Will you need to work with external partners?					

USE DATA TO BACK UP YOUR PLAN

You will need to frame your plan with data. This will enable you to sell the vision in presentations in order to get buy-in. Based on experience, it is prudent to spend time on the data that your plan is based on, even if the board's strategy is clear. It will give you a firm foundation to build on and enable you and your team to work better, faster and be more likely to succeed.

Keep it simple too. Do not over-complicate it. Your colleagues need to understand it, see where they fit in, what they will be required to do and why it is important for the business to change.

Data should be used in your plan to back up your decisions. With all of our interviewees across many sectors, data is driving decision-making, rather than managers acting on gut instinct, as was more the case in the past.

"To ground the conversation, you need to give them some facts", says Saswati Saha Mitra of her time at big tech company Google. She did a literature review just to frame a problem in India, where users were struggling with searches. She says she was "not even going into solution" at the planning stage.

So, learning how to act on data, which we will explore in Chapter 5, is vital. "You have to learn how to implement [data] for your planning process", says Michelle Senecal de Fonseca, a senior executive at Citrix, a US-based multinational software company.

WHO WILL HELP YOU?

Next, consider all the team dependencies – and who will help you solve the problem. The managers we spoke to collaborated with teams or key stakeholders across their organisations to create products or streamline ways of operating. They not only considered what they were trying to solve and why but also how quickly they were going to act and who would help them.

You may need to work with your team and discuss what elements need to be included because it is unlikely that you will be able to achieve success on your own. It is possible you will also need to collaborate with other departments. Make sure you have identified key stakeholders and gained their support because without it you are more likely to encounter obstacles, rather than having a clear runway. You may only need one or two people in each department to start building champions for change and they may include people who are new to the role or organisation and are keen to progress in their careers.

THOMAS STAMM

Team leader of innovation in editorial

What Thomas Stamm found when he was leading a digital transformation project at Neue Zürcher Zeitung (NZZ), a Swiss media company, was that the early adopters, the people willing to change, tended to get involved first. And a plan evolved.

"The natural change ambassadors were somehow involved in the project", says Stamm, who played a key role in transforming the company's shift from print to digital publishing, using technology to drive the project.

"A good tool can be a very strong enabler. That is what happened. The development of the tool involved a lot of important people driving change", he says.

His advice to other change agents is to draw up a plan first and "get people involved in a positive way".

"If you focus on doing the steps in the right order, then as a natural result, you look at processes, roles and tools. Look at what you want to achieve, what processes are best to get there and what roles are required to get this process in place and working", he says.

"Make a proper plan and do the first step first", he says. "You always have a lot of parallel things going on at the same time but don't try for short cuts initially."

The key to his success was focusing on following steps, one after the other, as part of a plan.

MAP OUT WHO TO CONTACT

Booster, a space tourism start-up, wanted to build a consortium of companies that would provide electronics, hardware, fuselage and control systems for a space tourism platform. It had to find out who was willing to be involved to give money, time or resources so that it could eventually do a test flight of an innovative vehicle over a commercial airport in Spain.

When it came to planning the project, it used a mind map, a visual representation of what it needed to do and who to contact to help.

Booster's core subject was 'design of spacecraft'. The team thought about all the elements or tasks that could link to it such as who would help them with each part of the project. They identified who they had to contact and why, as well as individual needs within the project objectives in order to bring them together and personalise communications. In this way, they successfully lobbied the government to achieve a vital outcome for the company: regulatory approval for test flights of an experimental vehicle. Once they had worked out who they needed to contact, they could move on to the next stage which was firming up commitments to be involved.

A mind map can help you explore your own team dependencies or key stakeholders that you will need to win over before you implement your plan. It is a good tool to use to break down your plan into smaller digestible pieces.

It will not only help to clarify your thoughts to deconstruct the problem but also visualise all the pieces that need to come together to make it work. Then you can attach people, skills, experiences and even organisations if necessary.

HOW TO CREATE A MIND MAP

1. First think of the core subject. This is the problem that needs solving.
2. Next, draw lines or branches from the core subject. Think about every team that needs to be involved in the transformation.
3. Write each team on each branch.

The following questions can guide you to figure out who these people are tactically:

■ What are all the options available to you? Which ones are viable?

■ Who are the key people to help you to influence others to create a 'cascade' effect?

■ Who has something to prove?

- ■ Who has credibility for subject expertise and would be willing to take a risk?
- ■ Are they willing to listen to a new narrative and help push it forward?
- ■ Will a senior leader help you to identify a middle manager who could be their representative?

It can be key where businesses begin the digital transformation process internally, because there will be knock-on effects across teams. Saswati Saha Mitra found this when she was working on the Google Search and Maps project.

It was also vital for Citrix. "For us, as a company, engineering was the key place to start because we needed to change our product and service", says Michelle Senecal de Fonseca, who was Area Vice-President at Citrix (Northern Europe) at the time of the interview.

"But when you change your product and service, there are new and different buyers to be considered, and how to sell to them changes.

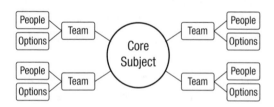

Figure 1.2 How to mind map

So the sales motion and our seller had to transform. Once you had the sales engine transform, then you start to realise your back office is not keeping pace so there is a knock-on effect", she says.

SASWATI SAHA MITRA

Research Leader at Whatsapp and former User Experience Researcher for Google Search and Maps

When Saswati Saha Mitra worked at Google, she was approached by the search engineering team, who had identified a problem in that users were not getting responses for the terms they searched for. "From a Google perspective, the problem was that they just didn't know why", she says.

It was a 'bit of a black box' as they could not figure out what was going on. There was no pre-existing data so they chose to look at the state of the internet in India, because that data was publicly available. They discovered there was a problem with the internet connection as many users were not even getting 4G bandwidth reliably half of the time.

But Mitra needed to find out what impact this had on people's experience of Google products. She led a multifunctional team of researchers, designers, engineers, product managers and data scientists to India, where the goal was to "get all of these people to think about the problem together, because none of us [on our own] would have been able to solve it".

Their research showed it was not only an internet issue but there were up to 16 different problems where searches were blocked. It affected not only Google Search but also YouTube, Maps, Chrome and Android.

In short sprints, they identified potential solutions. Mitra and her fellow researcher then discussed which ones were actionable with much of the leadership, which involved massive negotiation on what could be included in the roadmap.

"We would chase a VP of engineering down while he's out on a walk for ten minutes, give him the elevator pitch . . . This is why you need to know this. And then asking for a more detailed conversation", she says.

"I did almost 50 back-to-back meetings to get this notion of what is the real problem happening with users in India, out there, not only within the search organisation, but actually in YouTube, Google Maps, Chrome and Android. So these four teams [had] adjacencies with what we [were] doing."

She began to build the 'flywheel of momentum' where colleagues realised there was a problem and she gained their support.

In 2015, Google decided to invest in making all its products available offline, including YouTube and Chrome. Before this, there was no offline product. Today, you can use Google Maps offline and if you are on a poor connection, once it is restored, you will get the result back on Google search.

WHY SENIOR LEADERSHIP SUPPORT IS VITAL

As part of your planning process, it is important that you establish your mandate to make change happen. Even if you have been asked to lead a transformation project, you should be clear about your remit and how far it extends. This also means that while at the start you may have the support of senior leadership, which is key to your success as a change agent, you will need their backing to be continuous. You are likely to have to go back to senior champions many times to make your mandate clear because your status to carry out transformation can – and will – be challenged by other colleagues.

Prosci, a change management company, reported that in 2020 change leaders in 11 out of 11 studies identified effective executive sponsorship as the top contributor to success.

Without senior management's support, there is a risk of failure as you are likely to encounter hurdles and people will ask: Why you? They may even fail to make the connection between what you are doing and the strategic vision of the board – personalise the project rather than seeing it as part of a company-wide initiative to change.

Robert Shrimsley, Managing Editor of FT.com for ten years from 2009, spent the first year in the role securing leadership buy-in to change the FT's newsroom from focusing on the newspaper primarily to thinking about how to commission, edit and display stories visually on the website.

"I said to [the senior leadership]: 'We've got to step this up. Everybody's got to buy in and we've got to believe' and from the very beginning a core part of my first-year mission was making [the senior leadership] believe. I don't mean that [they] didn't because I was pushing at an open door. But I mean *really* buy-in."

Michelle Senecal de Fonseca at Citrix agrees. The direction "does need to come from senior leadership", she says, and it "has to be authentic" so that the rest of the organisation will commit.

Change agents should also be empowered to have the authority to cut across all the company's departments. If you are stuck in a silo "you will have limited effectiveness to the change that you're making", says Tom Fortin, Chief Operating Officer at iCapital Network and former Managing Director at BlackRock. "If you are empowered to cut across the organisation, and have the top-down empowerment, that's really important."

And as a team leader, you also "have to live and breathe it . . . [and] be the example", says Senecal de Fonseca. "You've got to participate in it and if you are uncomfortable then you have to go and find people who will help you. You've got to lead from the front as a manager."

As part of your plan, really think about how much transformation you can realistically achieve. While there may be pressure to deliver quickly, many of the change agents we spoke to told us the process can take a couple of years. Iberdrola took three years to plan their 11-year transformation project alone.

At the *Financial Times,* when newspaper production teams were merged and moved from a night to a day operation to streamline working processes and redeploy journalists into digital storytelling, the initial phase of producing a few print pages during the day happened quickly. But the entire change management phase took a couple of years to complete.

Since the pandemic in 2020, companies no longer have the luxury of time to deliver transformation. You may now have to turn operations around rapidly as organisations battle to survive.

You will also need to consider how much authority you have to make decisions. Sometimes there can be a point where you need more mandate from senior leadership. It is alright pushing you into the dragon's den but if you, as a manager, do not have the mandate to do certain things, colleagues start to think that you don't have the authority to make them do this or that. And this can start to become a real challenge, which we discuss in Chapter 2.

BE CLEAR ON THE WAY FORWARD

While SMART goals, derived from management theory developed by Peter Drucker, may be useful when setting clear goals and putting some structure on to your plan, they can be perceived as too rigid for the fast-paced business environment of today.

The CLEAR methodology, developed by Adam Kreek, a business coach and former Olympic rower, not only takes account of timeframes but also soft skills, such as emotional intelligence and collaboration, which are vital when making transformation projects work. It can also be used to build on the mind map.

The CLEAR acronym stands for:

C: Collaborate with your team and other stakeholders. This is key because no innovation project is done by one person.

L: Limit the scope and duration. Time lines are vital to gain momentum and avoid budget issues.

E: Emotional. Tap your passion and energy. Knowing yourself and being ready for the challenges ahead will always help to reach goals.

A: Appreciable. Break down goals into small steps. An important project can seem too overwhelming, so having bite-size steps can make it more realistic.

R: Refinable. Be ready to modify your plan. When you are doing something new for the first time, it is unlikely that you have all the answers at the start. You will have to update your approach according to what you learn and the new data gained on the journey.

It can help you to iterate along the way within a timeframe. By setting out your direction of travel, it will enable decision-making to be more efficient. You know where you want to get to, and how long it will take. This will help you to base decisions around that structure and succeed.

Break down your actions into smaller steps to come up with a structure. Think about short- and long-term goals. They may be for your team, department or at a company-wide operational level. You are setting out how your plan will work so it will need to include measurable objectives in a realistic timeframe. You are painting a picture of what the future is likely to hold and what you are aiming to achieve by that time.

CLEAR should be used as a tool to gain clarity and structure at the initial planning stage of an innovation project. It works because it brings in a broader and subtler scope of considerations which are often overlooked, such as your awareness of yourself regarding your passion and energy.

Innovation is hard work. If you are not prepared for it, how will others be ready?

EXERCISE

Use the CLEAR acronym to analyse the innovation challenge ahead as a checklist:

C: Identify team members and stakeholders who will support you and how.

L: Calculate the time needed for each milestone to keep motivation high and stay on time line and budget.

E: Consider your own readiness and if it is the right time for you and those who support you outside the office (especially your family) to embark on this change process as it may be an all-consuming task.

A: Identify milestones to be reached – when, with what resources and assets.

R: Add in checkpoints to appraise and discuss progress to make sure you are on track or to adjust in time.

KEEP IT FLEXIBLE

If you are attempting to break down departmental or team silos, bringing in structural change and cultural shifts in your organisation, you can edge your way to successful delivery by being flexible. Your plan should not be too rigid. You are likely to have to adapt it as you go because delivering transformation involves forming different habits, changing working practices, and adopting new ways of thinking, sometimes at speed. Innovation does not always run in a linear fashion, so be prepared for a possibly bumpy road. That may be a good mindset to start with.

Some companies form a skeleton structure in order to adapt it to circumstances and respond to unexpected outcomes. This can prove to be the most valuable of lessons and may even take the business in a different direction.

This was the experience of former Google executive Anastasia Leng when she co-founded her first business Hatch, a company that allowed consumers to customise any product, using 3D printing, have it made to order and shipped to them.

ANASTASIA LENG

Founder and Chief Executive of Hatch, a custom product site, and then CreativeX, a creative analytics software technology platform

Anastasia Leng did not plan much ahead with her first company, a custom product site, she co-founded in 2012. Originally called Makeably and later rebranded as Hatch, the former Google executive says that had they planned, they "would have realised this was not a great time to be in ecommerce".

"Our first business was very much driven by: 'Hey, this is really cool, let's go and build in'", she says. "If we had really sat down and planned ahead, we would have realised that this wasn't a viable long-term business."

With Hatch, she says the thesis they had to make ecommerce more adaptable was flawed – and it could have been improved with better planning.

"What we eventually learned, through lots of customer feedback, is that people care much more about having something that is good enough at a low enough price so that gratification can be fulfilled as quickly as possible. While what we were saying is that you can have exactly what you want but you will have to wait longer for it and probably pay more."

At Hatch, the financial planning could also have been more in-depth at the start. "If we had done that deeper financial planning to begin with, we probably wouldn't have pursued this business – or done it with a different business model behind it."

As Hatch tried to grow, the margins were small, the cost of acquisitions were high, and the company could not compete on ways to attract consumers, such as search ads, without significant venture capital investment.

"Essentially, we did everything wrong like many first-time founders. But I think it was an incredible experience because we got all those mistakes out of our system and we learned from them. When we launched our second company CreativeX we were able to get many things right from the start."

GET GOING

Having a structure can increase the likelihood of being successful because innovation is like an animal. It is very organic in the way it moves around all over the place.

"It is all about speed and getting going. You are never going to get perfection. If you seek perfection you will end up doing nothing because you can only do more research, more governance and more controls", says Mark Lillie at Deloitte.

Senior executives from sectors ranging from software to law firms agree with him. Michelle Senecal de Fonseca says you should be ready to adapt because "the metrics and the market are always constantly changing but then you are going to have to place your big bets – what are the key things you are going to have to get right and then you have to keep adapting underneath".

Michael Davison, Deputy Chief Executive at global law firm Hogan Lovells, says: "The bigger the organisation, the bigger the temptation to overplan. You can have great ideas but you can overthink them. You need to act on the lightbulb moment, just do it rather than let it fade."

"If . . . it takes six months to plan and implement, life has moved on."

Today, innovation cycles are much shorter than in the past and according to Senecal de Fonseca digital transformation is a "continuous lifestyle because just when you think you have gotten through one project you have to start on the next because the technology is escalating all of the time so you never really completely finish it. And that is really a little bit of a different outlook".

Companies are having to do a lot more of seeing what works, using the 'agile' management methodology, which we will look at in Chapter 3. This is where you come up with a hypothesis, you experiment, you go back and you reiterate and you keep trying. Then you get incremental change. This was how CNN's London newsdesk created a newsletter in 48 hours during the coronavirus pandemic.

BLATHNAID HEALY

Senior Director EMEA at CNN Digital International

The London newsdesk of CNN, a global news network, had to turn round a new product rapidly when it had to create a newsletter in hours during the pandemic in 2020. CNN Digital International is owned by CNN Worldwide, a unit of the Warner Media News & Sports division of AT&T's Warner Media.

It gained approval for the digital project late one evening. By the next morning the internal test was happening and the newsletter Coronavirus: Fact or Fiction *was emailed to inboxes later that evening, with the first public version published the following day.*

Having "very strong institutional knowledge of similar launches of newsletters that had months in the making" was key to the short planning stage succeeding, says Blathnaid Healy.

The product and editorial insights team members who had planned similar newsletters before were able to pour their expertise into a short time to work fast and guide colleagues. They were "key to condensing down those learnings and inputting them into some of us who were fresher to the scenario", Healy says.

"While we didn't have planning time and this is quite often the case with news . . . you have to have good relationships, good cross-functional relationships within teams. Then within your teams, you need people who are responsive and people who are going to thrive on the opportunity to do something." They must be self-motivated and "responsive to what is needed", she says.

As the newsletter was developed, graphics, logo and style were all added iteratively. But what began as a 'pop-up' newsletter – something that was to last for only a short time – was still running months later. This proved to be another learning point for managers who are thinking of drawing up a plan for a new product or innovation. Consider how you can support a project in the long term at the beginning, she says.

Another key skill was listening to expertise: "Going back to that phase and why we did what we did and how we did it: one of the things was getting a lot of smart people in a room is where a lot of these ideas come from", she says. Listening in a very cross-disciplinary manner from the various experts was key for the success of the newsletter, as well as collaborating on how best to reach the CNN audience.

Also, products do not last as long. They used to last a company ten years so you would not need to change work processes. Now, their life cycle is much shorter with upgrades required more frequently. This puts pressure on innovation to be fast because you might spend so much time and money on something that is ready in three years only for it to be already obsolete.

In this environment, it is not uncommon for business plans to emerge, especially where new technologies are being developed. This is what Thomas Stamm experienced at NZZ. He had a very rough start in 2014 when the Swiss media company declared at an organisational level that it would have one editorial team, merging print and online teams of journalists in the Zurich-based newsroom.

Although the intention behind the declaration from senior management was good, he says "it was an attempt to change the organisation without looking at the roles and processes" first in detail and this led to people feeling uncertain about what to do and who was responsible for what.

"The vision about where you are heading is not always precise and not always well understood and the technologies that are emerging continue to do so at pace", says Phil Neal, Digital Transformation Partner at Deloitte Digital in the UK.

Then you have to plough that furrow and take your team with you. It is likely to be tough at times as the path "is not always clear", he says.

But with your plan in place, you are more prepared for the way ahead and more likely to succeed.

WHAT TO DO NEXT

1. Make sure you have worked through the exercises, thinking about a real problem you need to solve for your customers.
2. Make a first draft of your plan.

3. Discuss your draft plan with the stakeholders you have identified. Add new perspectives and angles to avoid missing any important aspects and also actively involve people who you will need to execute it.

4. Be willing to be flexible, monitor progress and adapt if necessary.

FURTHER READING

Effective Planning and Time Management by Vivek Bindra

What's the Why by Simon Sinek

'Planning doesn't have to be the enemy of the agile' by Alessandro Di Fiore in *Harvard Business Review,* 13 September 2018

TED talk on 'The gap between planning and doing' by Kirsten Rohde, Professor of Behavioural economics at Erasmus University, Rotterdam

TED talk on 'A sixth sense for project management' by Tres Roeder, change agent and founder and President of Roeder Consulting

CHAPTER 2

CHALLENGES OF CHANGE: DEALING WITH THE DARK SIDE

As a change agent, you should expect to encounter resistance. You are likely to face pushback because conflicts, big or small, are normal during a transformation project, especially when people are worried about their roles changing or even losing their jobs.

We are calling it the 'dark side' because leading change can be so labour-intensive and exhausting. Dealing with transformation can take up a lot of your time and mental energy, so you will have to weigh the project up carefully to make sure it is worth it.

Here we will look at the type of challenges you are likely to face and how to prepare to deal with them. We will give you strategies to deploy to outwit the naysayers and win them over to changing their ways of working. The potential for clashes of opinion with colleagues who feel their roles are threatened or who just do not buy into the change is also all too real, with arguments breaking out as well as acts of defiance and possibly sabotage or even hostility.

Welcome to the challenges of innovation, where it takes courage and resilience from managers to navigate any conflict and opposition successfully. But be reassured that to succeed, it comes down to how the process is managed and how the workforce is supported throughout it.

WHY PEOPLE RESIST AND WHAT THEY DO

According to Tom Fortin, former Managing Director of BlackRock, transformation is "about the people. And if you ever forget it's about the people, you will always fail. Because in the end, it's not the technology that wins, it's the people that win". Tom Fortin has overseen some of the biggest transformation projects in the financial services sector.

Marta Javaloys, Global Design Lead who oversees transformation at Spanish bank BBVA, agrees: "Resistance to change is natural. And as human beings, we are wired to resist."

But if you can understand why people rebel against change, you stand a better chance of identifying potential conflict and mitigating against it.

There are four main reasons why resistance happens, according to a model by John Kotter and Leonard Schlesinger in their article 'Choosing strategies for change', published by *Harvard Business Review*.

SELF-INTEREST

Some staff are more concerned with the effects it will have on themselves rather than how it may help the business. It can have a lot to do with incentives, where employees may perceive the rewards of making the change do not compensate for the pain involved. This may be because they feel they have lost control over their territory and/or status, which can give rise to subtle political ways in which they will fight change.

"When people resist, it means something is blocking them from moving on, from evolving", says Javaloys at BBVA.

They can argue against initiatives, taking up their case with senior management if they are highly networked. They may be able to persuade other executives, who did not buy fully into the change project themselves, to take up their cause. They can also refuse to comply, failing to promote buy-in across their teams and undermine the project.

If they succeed in any of the above, they can delay change and hinder not only your progress but that of the business.

ANASTASIA LENG

Founder and Chief Executive of CreativeX, a creative analytics software technology platform

Anastasia Leng, who works with multinationals on transforming the way they make decisions about all their image and video content, finds that the resistance her company encounters is down to how the organisations she works with mitigates the risk.

"Every single company is capable of digital transformation if they want to do it. The question is do they want to do it and do they have the management structure and framework by which they can roll this out successfully. We've seen some companies do this exceptionally well", she says.

One of these is Unilever, a consumer goods maker, she has worked closely with. That multinational group thought openly about where it was going to see resistance to this and how it could get "in front of that", she says.

A common resistance path for CreativeX, for example, is when the company suddenly brings visibility around how effective partners have been at making a concept happen.

Telling them which of their agency partners are doing well and which of them are not is a "tricky proposition" and employees often "push back on that", out of self-interest.

▶

Unilever "was great at anticipating that", she says. It collaborated with CreativeX to draw up a plan on rolling out changes to working practices, explaining across the company how this was going to be good for everyone's benefit, and getting all the agency partners on board. At the time, CreativeX thought about how to communicate across an organisation that probably has thousands of partners.

"Unilever is a very good partner and very thoughtful about the way it rolls out new technology across the board", she says, so CreativeX was "able to sail smoothly through that".

CreativeX has seen other companies not be so successful at rolling out change programmes. What happens then is that "it is less successful for everyone".

This is usually the case when the senior leadership has not bought into the transformation idea. "You could have a company where you have one person who is excited about this and thinks that is the way they should be operating. [But] they might not have the authority to do this. They might not have the ear of the senior people to do this", she says.

POOR COMMUNICATION

Misunderstandings can arise due to a lack of information and unclear communication. Decisions can be perceived as being imposed, with teams having little input or consultation.

A shortage of time to get used to the idea of transformation and digest what it means for their careers can also lead to rejection. This tends to occur if plans have been drawn up in secret and lack transparency. Typically in this situation, trust will be low between managers and employees.

It takes a brave person to make a very clear statement at the beginning and for most people to actually believe in it. And if that important interaction is lacking, the situation starts to become political – and when it is political it becomes emotional. When that happens, it can be very difficult to deal with and can escalate into conflict. This is when external mediators may be asked to step in.

FEAR OF THE UNKNOWN

Psychologically, some employees have a low tolerance to change because security and stability are key for them. People typically try to avoid fear and uncertainty. "I think the most relevant part is the fears that people have, regarding what the new situation may bring, and if it makes them feel in danger", says Javaloys at BBVA.

Certain employees will not be able to adapt to the new scenario and they will perceive the change as a threat. "It's something that organisationally needs to be managed", she says.

This may be partly down to how hard it is to change habits. What tends to happen is that businesses evolve but processes may not and while they become outdated, people will still be working in an inefficient way.

Tom Fortin, Chief Operating Officer of iCapital Network, a financial technology platform, experienced this during his career in the asset management industry, as did Anastasia Leng, founder of CreativeX, when she worked with external partners on transformation projects.

"People are irrational creatures and don't like change. Someone has been doing something in a certain way for the last ten years and now you are telling them to do it differently. Even if it is objectively better, it never feels like it is better, because it's different", says Leng.

This type of behaviour is seen even in some parts of Japan Inc, for example, where resistance to digitisation is so strong that some companies are still using floppy disks, the computer memory storage devices first sold almost 50 years ago. The use of paper-based systems by Japanese financial institutions and their clients is still widespread, Tatsufumi Sakai, Chief Executive of Mizuho, a Japanese bank, told *Financial Times* in 2020.

At the FT itself, when the newsroom was trying to encourage journalists to think 'digital-first', that change of mindset took a long time. "It wasn't that people were obstructive. But the changes were not their natural default so people reverted back to the way they were", says Robert Shrimsley, the then Managing Editor of FT.com.

"Some big story would break and you would hear the conversation over the newsdesk about what they were going to do: 'We've got a fast take-up for the web that will be updated.'

"Then their hands would go up and they would start to draw the page [in the air]: 'We are having an analysis, a profile. . . ' And you would watch them – they were still thinking totally newspaper."

TOM FORTIN

Former Managing Director at BlackRock

"I used to say my job was to make people do things they don't want to do", says Tom Fortin, who not only worked on integrating the BlackRock acquisitions of

Merrill Lynch investment managers in 2006–08 but also Barclays' global investors from 2009–13.

"People can be your allies and instructors to change but others can be passive aggressive, especially if you do not focus on them and what the transformation means for them", he says.

"In some cases, the business process has not changed for 15 years and people are still operating in the same way as when they started the company.

"They are working like a cook, who, in an allegory, had always cut off the last one third of some beef before putting it in a pan to roast. They continued to work this way even when they had a bigger pan which would easily accommodate all the meat. When asked why they did this, they said it was because they used to have a small pan and used to have to cut a portion of the meat off.

"That story always resonated because it's what people do", says Fortin. When he was looking to streamline processes at a business group in the asset management industry, he encountered a team that was reluctant to change the way they worked. The group was running $800 billion of funds and allocating new cash flows into these funds, no matter how small the trade because the clients had been promised there would never be any cash in the portfolio.

"So [the team] had to invest every dollar, every last penny", he says. But what this meant was it might cost $10 to process a trade that was only 10 cents in size.

Fortin drilled down into the processes and the data behind them, and realised cash was already going to be in the portfolio because the funds pay dividends. He used the data to bust the 'myth' that there was never any cash in the portfolio.

"All of a sudden, everyone's like: 'Oh, maybe we can reconsider what we're doing,'" he says.

He analysed more data to find out how many times they were allocating less than $100 to billion-dollar funds. This showed it was 30 per cent of every trade so they stopped doing the small trades. "We cut 30 per cent of all the trading out", he says, making the business more efficient.

"The only way you really get to business transformation is to understand the process, the business purpose, the upstream contributors, the downstream dependencies, and then use data and facts, to break the myths that people have about what they do and why they do it", he says.

DIFFERENT VIEWPOINTS AND LACK OF FORESIGHT

It is common for workers to see the reason for change differently. They may disagree on the pros and cons of change and may see more costs than benefits not only to them but also to the business. Or perhaps senior leadership lacks vision or foresight of where the business should be heading. There are many famous examples of this, such as US film producer Darryl Zanuck dismissing the idea of television in 1946. The world would become tired of "staring at a plywood box" every night, he said. Then there was Thomas Watson, President of IBM in 1943, who said: "I think there is a world market for maybe five computers."

That type of thinking was not confined to the 1940s. In 2008, Jim Keyes, chief executive of video rental chain Blockbuster, told The Motley Fool, a US financial services website: "Neither RedBox nor Netflix are even on the radar screen in terms of competition. It's more Walmart and Apple", he said. Blockbuster filed for bankruptcy in 2010.

Among colleagues, though, you may encounter a perception that a project is just the latest iteration in a transformation programme and that it will fade away given time.

This is something that Abe Smith, Head of International at Zoom, has seen at other companies: "One of the challenges I found at other organisations is that as much as you wanted to help the customer, there were boundaries. I think care is fundamentally important to overcome these challenges and provide the best possible customer service."

Sometimes one part of the business can have a view of the way forward and make a digital change only for other regions in the same company to trail behind.

At Rio Tinto, an Anglo-Australian mining group, the commercial legal team based in Singapore started thinking about digital transformation from the perspective of their clients and how they wanted to buy iron ore. The team digitalised their mining contracts, reducing the number of pages needed from 100 to 15.

They took a customer-centric approach and simplified the language so they could all be signed on WeChat, a mobile phone ecommerce and chat platform, because that was what their top Chinese customers were demanding. That's according to Reena SenGupta, of UK-based RSG Consulting, a specialist research and consulting company with decades of experience analysing the legal industry. "It happened really quickly and doubled the amount of iron ore they could sell", she says.

The Asia-Pacific region won an innovative lawyers award in 2020 for transforming the way they worked.

But even in an advanced corporate legal team, the rates at which it digitally transforms is not uniform. "Different jurisdictions have different cultural approaches. For example, some US legal teams are more resistant to digital. It is not uncommon to find them using Lotus Notes or deeply questioning whether legal will derive any value from being digital", says SenGupta. "Many see the legal profession – lawyers and what they do – as intrinsically different. It is a profession based on precedent, and there is no precedent for digital in legal. It took a pandemic to get lawyers to wholescale accept electronic signatures."

CONFLICT AND COUPS

'Volatile, Uncertain, Complex and Ambiguous' (VUCA) was a phrase coined by the US Army to describe warfare but it can be used as a metaphor to describe change projects which can feel like a type of war. You can find yourself engaged in typical 'dark-side' behaviour, such as people being passive aggressive, performing tasks slowly in a pressured, deadline-driven environment and refusing to pick up work, or colleagues expressing their views in a forthright way, even if it causes arguments and conflict. Sometimes this can really build up, with people storming out of the office and even lead to attempted coups to topple managers.

One person who has had to deal with things that go wrong is Anne Boden, who founded Starling, a digital bank in the UK. The former Chief Operating Officer of Allied Irish Bank wrote about her journey and setbacks with Starling in her book *Banking on it: How I disrupted an industry,* with one chapter titled 'Near-death experience'.

In the book, she describes how, after a key investment deal fell through, she was stunned when the then Chief Technology Officer abruptly resigned. Members of the senior management team also left with him and at one point she faced 'nothing less than a coup' when they went to set up a rival challenger bank, which would go on to become Monzo.

ANNE BODEN

Chief Executive and founder, Starling, UK challenger bank

"As a team, we'd been through so much at Starling: ups, downs, extreme triumphs and crushing blows. We'd weathered them all. We'd been stressed almost to breaking point at times, but we'd got through it. What had changed now?" she wrote.

It was a big news story at the time in 2015. When members of her senior leadership team quit suddenly the future of the challenger bank was in doubt.

"What happened to me was humiliation", she says. "It was all over the newspapers . . . that evening, I had a dinner. And I can still feel it, I can still actually see my footsteps walking into the restaurant and figuring out how I was going to face people. And, you know, I can still see the people around the table and, and what people said and how I felt. But I went to that dinner, I got dressed up, put my make-up on and I survived.

"But let's just put it in proportion. It wasn't life and death. I wasn't going to starve, right. And it was just dealing with my thoughts and thoughts about myself. And my image in other people's eyes. And I think you have to keep that distinction."

One of the techniques that got her through that period was how she managed herself and drew on her resilience. "There's a technique in realising that you feel like that at that moment. And it is very, very intense when it's happening. But . . . things change. And it's a question of dealing with it at the moment. And then being there the following day, to carry on", she says. "Resilience is really a muscle that you exercise, and you get better at it."

"If things are really, really tough, and I really have to do something really difficult, I think that you can turn that negative emotion and negative pressure into positive action to try and change that. I've gone through tough times, and I've survived, and I've gone on to do something more interesting", she says.

EXERCISE

1. *Consider the four main reasons why people resist change and identify which ones may apply to your team members.*

2. *Write down who you should speak to and plan to ask them what would make them be on board with the transformation project.*

3. *If you work in a consensus-driven culture, try generating solutions by brainstorming with each resistant team member individually to help them take a different approach. If this feels overwhelming and you have a large team, move on to 4.*

4. *Initiate open dialogue with your whole team by holding weekly meetings with the purpose for staff to air any issues in a constructive way. Proactively encourage them to get in touch if they have any concerns.*

Who is a crucial stake-holder?	Why are they resistant?	What is their level of resist-ance?	What is their level of influence?	What are your options?	Who will support you?

Figure 2.1 Resistance template

Adapted from What is a Change Resistance Management Plan, and what are best practices, tools and online templates for teams and organisations.

Using the steps above to analyse your situation, in the template above fill each column with the answers requested.

In this way you can build a structured approach to how to deal with resistant team members with a detailed action plan. Going person by person, you will gain new insights and approaches on how to move the project forward.

WHAT YOU CAN DO

Managers can influence resistance to change in several ways and have positive outcomes. There is unlikely to be one answer that fits all and in reality you will find that you will use a mixture of tactics to suit the situation you face. You can prepare by devising your own tailor-made strategy to anticipate problems and how to resolve them, rather than attempting to tackle them in an incremental way.

Kotter and Schlesinger suggested six approaches that can help to tackle their four reasons why people resist. You can help to reduce tension and mitigate the risk of rebellion by doing a mixture of the following:

■ Communicate

■ Involve and support

■ Negotiate and agree

WHAT TACTICS TO USE

The following approaches have not only worked in our experience but also at the companies we spoke to. We would recommend that you draw up your own strategy using a mix of these tactics from the start of a project to suit the situation you face:

■ Communicate throughout the process often and repeatedly to sell your vision and promote understanding of it that will lead to buy-in.

■ Involve and support. Actively listen to other ideas and seek colleagues' perspectives. They may have seen other ways to make improvements.

■ Negotiate and seek agreement. It is important for all stakeholders to be clear about the benefit for them.

TACTIC 1: COMMUNICATE

You just cannot communicate enough during a period of transformation. You can never have too many individual conversations, team or larger departmental meetings and wider 'town halls' that are open to the whole company. All of these will not only be repeating the message but also educating the workforce about why change is necessary and giving the context to everyone about where the business is heading. As a change agent, you will play your part in reinforcing this message. By setting out the case for change, it can help to avoid conflict.

Clear statements are easily understood but have to be made with authenticity and empathy for them to be accepted and generate motivated action. It is better to over-communicate, to foster more dialogue and engagement. In this way, team members establish open and frequent communication which helps to create bonds and clarify doubts.

Individual conversations can help to defuse any potential conflict in a company setting but it can depend on the context of what you are trying to do. If people are not dependent on each other for interaction over work, it is probably easier to have one-to-one talks.

Simon Sinek, a management consultant and author, said in a TED Talk that the 'why' (or context) was critical in not only developing powerful company value propositions but also in creating a motivated team who believe in what they are doing. He talked about the 'golden circle' of 'What, How, Why'.

In his book *Start with Why,* Sinek wrote that every organisation knows what they do and some know how they do it, but few know why they exist. But if they do know, it "is a purpose, cause or belief". Also, messages that concentrate on emotions, behaviour and decision-making are more effective at the neurological level.

"Have an understanding of why this [change] is a good thing and what aspects are difficult about it and then communicate it in as many ways as possible", says Sarah Wells, Technical Director for Operations and Reliability at the *Financial Times.* "Even where change is difficult, you have to really feel this is the right thing, otherwise you can't sell it to people."

Meri Williams, former Chief Technology Officer at challenger bank Monzo, agrees. She tries to get people on side by explaining the 'why' to colleagues, to help educate them on the logic for change. "If there is no Why, or nobody will share with them the Why . . . they are going to resist either actively or passively because they are not going to do things for the sake of doing them", she says.

Then you have to keep pushing the message home because "people don't necessarily catch it the first time you say it", says Wells. They can be busy doing other things or they simply did not read the email properly.

"You have to send things again and again and say it in lots of different ways so that people really understand it. And you will still have people turning round and saying: 'I didn't know this was happening'. And you can turn round and say well you got an email and there was a Slack message and it was announced at this meeting", she says.

Nico Arcauz at Iberdrola agrees that strong communication is vital. When he oversaw a transformation project, newsletters were used in an education drive to disseminate information to about 4,000 employees so they could understand the direction of travel for the company.

"You achieve something magical about it when the whole organisation buys into the project. That is certainly a challenge and I don't have an easy answer for that. Just call Harry Potter and ask him to work his magic because it is not easy at all", he says.

In another editorial project at the *Financial Times* in 2013, transforming the newsroom from a mainly print-focused operation to a digital one, meetings ranging from individual conversations and team discussions to company-wide town halls, and consultations with the National Union of Journalists were held regularly.

Communication was key because the culture was one of consensus. No one was being forced to change. But individuals needed to be convinced to make the move from a four-night a week working pattern to five days and teams needed to be assured of the business reasons by senior managers. And it paid off in the long term with many colleagues deciding to make the change.

IN SUMMARY

- Understand why the transformation is necessary.
- Explain the logic of any decisions.
- Acknowledge which aspects are difficult.
- Communicate in as many ways as possible.

FRANK DE WINNE

Former Commander of International Space Station (ISS) Expedition 21

While astronauts have specific psychological profiles and are put through a rigorous selection process, managers can learn some lessons from the type of training they undergo.

Given the confined and isolated environment in space, astronauts are taught to spot early signs of tensions arising or if some of the crew members are not happy or withdrawing.

"Conflict is always something that builds up – so what are the early signs and what can you do to reduce the tension before it reaches a conflict?" asks Frank De Winne, who is now the European Space Agency ISS Programme Manager, and the second Belgian in space.

▶

When he served as commander of ISS Expedition 21, he made sure the crew always had their meals together as much as possible so that you could discuss anything that happened during the day and look at whether any adjustments needed to be made to the way they were operating. This was a moment where "it was not stressful" and they could listen to music together. They rotated who chose the music every night to "create a group dynamic".

This was important because when he arrived at the space station, he and two other astronauts who had flown with him, joined three other crew members who were already there.

"When you come to the space station you have to integrate with the team that is already there", he says. "On board, they have their dynamics so you have to integrate to that." Then there is a rollover, where those three people leave and three new ones come in. "Then the dynamics of the team changes because if you change 50 per cent of the team composition the dynamic changes."

Culturally, the crew were very different, often comprising Russians, Americans, Europeans and Japanese. "But all the people have the same goal. They want to fly into space and they want to make the best out of their mission . . . So of course it is easier to manage", he says.

TACTIC 2: INVOLVE AND SUPPORT

Encourage people to participate because they may spot ways to improve the process. Listening to their ideas and using their suggestions can help because it starts to give them ownership and they may begin to commit to the cause. By giving them a voice, it can make them feel validated and appreciated.

"Giving people end-to-end ownership leads to the best outcome", Meri Williams, former Chief Technology Officer at Monzo, says.

You can also give people responsibility for helping you drive the change. This may lead to long-term buy-in. But this method does have drawbacks. It can be very time-consuming and it will have to be managed carefully. It is also important to make clear what can or cannot be realistically done to avoid frustration if you decide not to use their suggestions.

As part of facilitation, you can act like a 'bridge' where you either walk alongside people to help them across or push them along to enforce change.

Overseeing the implementation of the broadcast schedule in editorial at the FT took a lot of labour-intensive work, supporting colleagues through how to make their stories transparent by using a software programme that was poorly adopted at the time.

You can also use selective information to try to effect change. At the FT, when the broadcast schedule, a transparent list of stories with their publication times, was launched, some heads of newsdesks were reluctant to embrace it because they saw it as more work for them and their teams.

But a couple of people within these teams who were open to change were asked to take part in the 'secret' project and under no circumstances to tell their managers about it. Within 48 hours, those managers were demanding to be part of the so-called secret project and were only too willing to help make it work.

While some colleagues may actually never cross the bridge and will leave the company, others may stay and continue to resist.

"In any change you do not bring everyone along with you and I do think you have to recognise that", says Sarah Wells, who has overseen different transformation projects in the IT department at the FT. "If you work in IT you might be able to move on because you don't like the change here and now, but in ten years' time it would have happened everywhere."

"There's a part where you need to understand that certain people in certain contexts are not going to change", says Marta Javaloys at BBVA. "You need to manage your energy to understand what part of the context you just need to accept and where you have space to facilitate change and make an impact."

Competency issues can also come into play here where colleagues feel they do not have the required skills to thrive. They may be concerned they will be forced to work in a different way and they will not be able to succeed. They could also be feeling anxious about whether the workload will rise, resulting in them being asked to do more with fewer resources as well as increasing the likelihood of making mistakes.

"You need to understand what people's context, needs, fears and barriers are and build that picture to find allies and to build a shared vision of where you want to go", says Javaloys. "What does [the transformation] actually mean to people in their daily lives?"

If they do not feel supported, it is likely the project may not work.

WHEN TO ENFORCE

There will also be some element of enforcement – and that can sit in your role as a change manager.

A way of applying pressure on non-compliant teams is to start with those who volunteer to do things differently and slowly surround the resisters with change agents.

Tom Fortin uses this strategy to bring teams around to new ways of working. He calls it the 'surround, humiliate' plan. He would identify the teams most open to change – they may have offered to run a project, for example – and get them to successfully transform business practices.

"Then I would go down the line of transferring and transitioning the next teams. And at the end, if there were six teams, five of them would transition", he says. That sixth team would still be using the old system but they would have to own all of its costs. He would also give them the power to decide whether they wanted to change – and they did. "That was a painful process to make sure that you'd captured it. But that was absolutely key to doing it", he says.

At the FT, there were often arguments around bringing copy deadlines forward by 24 hours to publish copy for 5am to meet the peak audience online. It was a way to streamline print production processes and redeploy staff into digital roles.

This project took a level of daily enforcement for something like close to two years for the new ways of working to become ingrained.

IN SUMMARY

- Encourage staff to improve processes.
- Listen to their ideas and give them a voice so they start to take ownership.
- Give them responsibility for helping you with delivery.
- Act like a bridge between strategic vision and reality at the coalface.
- Enforce change when necessary.

TACTIC 3: NEGOTIATE AND AGREE

Negotiated agreements can avoid major action against proposed change. It is sometimes easy to forget the role of unions who can be 'friend or foe' depending on the circumstance. They can help to support change or hinder it if they feel that it is not in the benefit of their members. It is vital to factor in the importance of unions and consider how you approach them if they are in your workplace and it is within your remit to do so.

At the FT, the consultations with the National Union of Journalists (NUJ) were labour-intensive and it took about 18 months to achieve a consensus-driven outcome. But it did avoid any large-scale confrontation.

On an individual level, a person may be motivated by many things such as power, job retention, prestige, or access to new information. By understanding the benefit for each person involved, you may be able to motivate the team by negotiating incentives, if you have the authority to do so.

It is important for stakeholders to understand what is the win for them – and it is likely to be different for each one. Do not take it for granted that, for example, the company is funky, innovative and going to change the world. There is something underneath that.

Even though there is a clear goal for the company, people can interpret that in different ways. For some it may be about prestige or power, and for others financial gain or a chance to learn something new. Knowing what their motivations and needs are can help to identify what it will take to win them over to the project.

Most people stay with the status quo but to make change happen you need them to step up. Some will do this naturally but many would prefer to stay as they are unless you can find the benefit for them.

Much conflict comes out of a lack of a deeper understanding of team members' 'needs', which are specific and actionable. This is different to their 'wants', which tend to make people take sides and enter into a blame game. One way of looking at this is by using a classic example from the world of mediation. In the 'orange dispute', two people fight for a piece of fruit and you have to help them to find a solution. In conflict, the parties tend to be short-sighted and cannot see beyond the dispute.

What do you do here? You could offer solutions such as buying another orange and cutting it in half. But we do not know if this is possible or even if it is what the parties want. If we ask why, something else could happen. 'Why': let's us understand what is important for the parties and what their real needs are.

In this case, one says: "I need the orange peel to make a cake for my colleague." The other says: "I need the pulp to make orange juice as I have a cold coming on."

Now we have discovered that the needs are complementary and we found a solution through asking the right question. We have gone from a position, to understanding the underlying interests, to an actionable need.

But this tactic needs to be handled in a measured way because it is easy to become emotional in tough situations. A working agreement with a group of people tasked with a mission can help you to focus on their needs, aligning values and behaviours from the start and help to mitigate resistance. It can be effective in helping you to discover and share much new information in your team and have a powerful 'inside conversation' which gets to the nub of their interests and needs.

You will then be able to use it to form the base of a team mission statement and it can become a living document that can be referred back to and adjusted as you go along and learn more about each other through the project. It will also help to create a solid team foundation when time is of the essence as well as when much work is carried out remotely, mitigating risk and creating buy-in.

To do this, we have to go beyond subjective 'banner words', such as respect and trust, which are usually what people say when asked which values and behaviours are important at work. Each party has to explain what the words mean for them. As an example, for one person the most important aspect of respect could be arriving on time to meetings. For another, it could mean having open and frequent communication. This leads us to discovering actionable needs.

IN SUMMARY

- Negotiate agreements and incentives if possible.
- Understand the benefit for each individual involved.
- Identify what it will take to win over staff.
- Draw up a working agreement to align values and behaviours to mitigate risk.

WHAT NOT TO DO

We believe a couple of approaches that Kotter and Schlesinger list are high risk and stand a chance of backfiring:

- Manipulation and co-optation
- Explicit or implicit coercion

In manipulation you use selective information to influence the behaviour of naysayers. In co-optation, you ask respected leaders to take part in shaping the transformation programme, but do not give them any real power to make decisions.

Meanwhile, in coercion, you either explicitly threaten people to force them to change. Perhaps they could lose their jobs, be transferred or fail to be promoted. Or you make suggestions, implying the likely negative impact on the business if they fail to adopt new ways of working.

Both strategies can lead to a lack of buy-in and should only be used where the speed of change makes it necessary.

EXERCISE

This is a good follow-on activity to build on the previous exercise. It can help teams gain a deeper understanding of each member as they work on business needs together and move towards the creation of a common mission statement.

It is a group exercise to understand your team better and it will need some time, possibly two hours for a team of five. A colleague should act as note-taker.

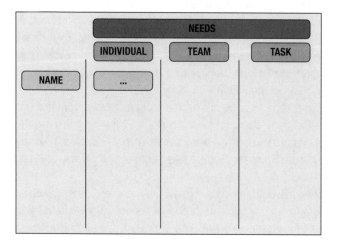

Figure 2.2 'Needs of your team' template

Use the template above to work out the needs of your team by doing the following:

1. *Ask each team member to come up with key words for each column. They should do this on their own so they are not influenced by others because you want to know what is important for each person. For 'Individual', it is what others need to know about how they prefer to work. For 'Team', it is what they expect from their group. For 'Task', it is to share their ideas of how to organise the work, based on their experience. For this, set aside ten to 15 minutes.*

2. *Once each person has thought about the main words for each column (usually five to eight items), they convene to share and explain what they mean to them, going beyond the 'banner words'. It is recommended they each speak for a few minutes, so that everyone takes part from the outset, and then discuss the findings as a group.*

This type of conversation can be very powerful as it leads to much discovery and new information that can help the team form closer bonds, understand intentions and find better ways to work and communicate.

WHEN TO CALL IN THE MEDIATORS

Finally, if conflict continues to escalate, a company may choose to hire mediators to help resolve the dispute and rebuild relationships. They are typically brought in when employees feel aggrieved, usually by one or more team members, to coach them so that they can communicate together. If the company has a strict behaviour policy, a team member can also refer to that to request mediation.

The advantage for a company is that its reputation remains unaffected because the issue does not become public. Mediation is widely used but depends on country and company culture. If it works, it can help to improve organisational practices. But if it fails, legal action usually still remains an option.

A mediator would normally explain why they are dealing with whatever the issue is to set the context. Individual conversations would be held with everyone to understand what was important for each person and how they saw it as well as looking objectively at the facts. Findings from these conversations would be collected anonymously and discussed openly to go forward.

If there were particular issues between certain people, the mediators would facilitate those conversations between them. All successful mediations finish with an agreement and follow up plan signed by all parties.

WHAT TO DO NEXT

1. Create a culture of open and constant communication by initiating individual and group meetings.

2. Understand individual motivations and needs to tailor your approach giving each team member a reason to help with the change process.

3. Be open to external help if it is needed because it will demonstrate it is important for you as a manager to progress.

FURTHER READING

Start with Why by Simon Sinek

'Ten reasons people resist change' in *Harvard Business Review* by Rosabeth Moss Kanter, Rosabeth Moss Kanter, 25 September 25 2012

The Catalyst: how to change anyone's mind by Jonah Berger

Leading Change by John Kotter (audiobook)

Transforming resistance to change with Christine Comaford (podcast)

CHAPTER 3

EXERCISING THE AGILITY MUSCLE

B y taking a page from the start-up playbook, managers can learn from and adapt entrepreneurial approaches to apply them to their own innovation projects. Experimenting, iterating and coming up with creative solutions to problems all help to scale quickly. In the start-up world, small, incremental steps are taken, reviewed and modified to respond to changing business needs.

On the other hand, traditional companies typically plan for two to five years and, before the coronavirus pandemic in 2020, took time to adapt or react to change. At the Financial Times, some newsroom digital transformation projects took about two years to fully embed, for example.

Here we explore what you can learn from a start-up approach and how you can apply it.

Most companies we spoke to, from education providers and online retailers to global media and financial services companies, were iterative in practice rather than in ambition, getting a project off the ground quickly and scaling up as it progressed and proved successful.

This was seen more generally during the pandemic, when innovation cycles shortened and the pace of work accelerated across all sectors in a battle for business survival. It took Ineos, the chemicals group, for example, just ten days to build hand-sanitiser plants in Germany and the UK in 2020.

"Such energy is more usually associated with tech start-ups, which are driven by their potential. As companies grow bigger, this energy can be lost. Now is an opportunity for all to rediscover and harness it", Amanda Murphy, HSBC UK Head of Commercial Banking, wrote in the Sunday Times.

While in the banking sector, even before the pandemic, challenger rivals were "without a doubt on the radar of the established banks, who are clearly watching our every move and innovation like hawks", Anne Boden, founder of digital bank Starling, wrote in her book Banking on it: How I Disrupted an Industry. "While the big banks are playing catch-up, we're innovating all the time, staying one, two or several steps ahead" because start-ups are "fleet of foot", she wrote.

WAYS TO ADAPT AND LEARN

We have chosen to highlight the three methodologies of Kaizen, Lean and Agile because in our experience and interviews with close to 50 companies, these were the most widely used terms. All three of them are broad but similar ways of coming up with a significant outcome for a business, putting adaptability and learning at their heart. Any company can apply the thinking to grow their business.

But some managers may be hard-pressed for time to work out which one to use. And yet it is important to have an insight into how these methodologies can help you and your team to innovate. Otherwise you may risk a 'half-hearted implementation' that will most probably fail, and "every failure makes the next attempt even less likely to succeed", according to an article on LinkedIn, the professional networking website.

WHAT IS KAIZEN?

Kaizen is a concept that was developed to help rebuild the Japanese economy after the second world war but it is known today as a way to enhance efficiency and quality with the help of staff. It is based on two pillars:

- Continuous improvement
- Respect for people and teamwork

A well-known example of its application includes the Toyota Way where any worker at the car-maker could stop a process if they saw an abnormality and suggest an improvement.

It "is a way of thinking which encourages and empowers everyone to identify where and how even small changes can be made to benefit the business, their team or their individual performance", according to Toyota's website. Instead of choosing, for example, between two big projects, you can ask all stakeholders to become involved and check progress in small steps as you move forward with the project.

It has become the basis of both lean and agile management theories, which originated in the world of software development in the US, and are also about delivering constant iteration.

WHAT IS LEAN?

Lean is about learning what your customers want, testing continuously, then adapting and adjusting, wrote entrepreneur Eric Ries in his book *The Lean Start-up.* He outlines five principles of the method:

1. **Entrepreneurship:** Includes anyone who has to create products and services under extreme uncertainty. "That means entrepreneurs are everywhere and the Lean Start-up approach can work in any size company, even a very large enterprise, in any sector or industry", he wrote.

2. **Entrepreneurial management:** A new kind of leadership style with internal innovators (intrapreneurs) who thrive in volatile times.

3. **Validated learning:** Run experiments to test the vision.

4. **Build, measure, learn:** Turn ideas into products, measure how customers respond, pivot or persevere.

5. **Be accountable:** Focus on how to measure progress, how to set up milestones and how to prioritise work.

The core idea behind lean "is to maximise customer value while minimising waste", an article said on the website www.lean.org. Eliminating waste creates more efficient processes that need less human effort, less space, less capital and less time to make products and services with fewer costs and fewer defects than traditional methods, it said.

For example, Inditex, the biggest clothing retailer which operates in 93 markets globally, incorporates lean methodology in Zara, its flagship fashion chain, to increase quality and efficiency in production and warehousing processes. The benefit of using lean was seen during the pandemic in particular when Bloomberg reported that Inditex's 'quick-reaction strategy' allowed the operator of Zara stores to reduce inventory in the middle of lockdowns, buoying first-half earnings.

WHAT IS AGILE?

Agile is an iterative way to deliver value to customers quickly and respond to changing business needs through collaboration with multidisciplinary teams. It originated in 2001 from the 'Twelve principles of the Agile Manifesto', drawn up by a group of software developers in the US, and it starts by saying it is helping to uncover better ways of developing software. Other principles include:

- **Iterate:** Welcome changing requirements even late in the day.
- **Collaborate:** Trust colleagues to get the job done with self-organising teams.
- **Pay continuous attention:** To technical excellence to enhance agility.
- **Reflect:** Then refine and adjust.

Now it is an approach used beyond the technology sector to other industries such as telecoms, banking and even mining and oil and gas, according to an article on McKinsey's website. Agile models aim "to get an early prototype of a new product or service out into customers' hands as quickly as possible", the report says.

Projects are usually taken in small steps, with requirements, plans and results evaluated continuously so any response to change is quick.

The leadership style in these teams is to collaborate and self-organise as the team is best placed to know how to deliver the project based on its resources and constraints.

HOW ARE THE THREE MODELS SIMILAR?

All three methodologies have been used in fast-paced businesses that have limited resources to innovate and can either be applied in an organic, impro-vised way or with a more structured approach. They have many similarities, according to McKinsey, when it comes to improving business systems:

- Delivering value efficiently for customers.

- Continuously learn and improve.

- Connect strategy and goals to give teams purpose.

- Enable people to contribute.

All of them focus on the idea of using small steps with all stakeholders involved to make better and faster decisions that improve production and other processes.

Choosing between Kaizen, lean and agile

Method	Keys	Pros	Cons	When to use
Kaizen	Continuous improvement	Increases product quality	Distorts management system	To build employee engagement
Lean	Increase efficiency	Optimises resources	Causes stress	To foster a 'testing mindset'
Agile	Self-managing teams	Enhances flexibility	Hard to predict	To quicken team adaptation

For the purposes of this book, we believe the main point is that, regard-less of which method you choose, by taking an incremental approach and regularly reviewing progress, you can adapt your plan when necessary. A

McKinsey report backs up this thinking: "The mistake we find many leaders and organisations making is believing they need to choose between [agile and lean]. In fact, that's not true. Not only is choosing unnecessary, but the two methodologies complement one another in ways that increase the impact they generate, often by deploying . . . technologies to speed transformation."

This view was supported by many of the companies we spoke to. As Meri Williams, former Chief Technology Officer at challenger bank Monzo found in her experience, it did not really matter which approach companies used, but whether they were "inspecting and adapting" how they worked. "A lot of places think they are transforming by going agile but if they are not testing and learning, inspecting and adapting, it is a huge red flag to me if you have multiple teams and they all use the same process", she says.

Next we have cherry-picked best practice of elements of these three methodologies.

TRY FIRST

It can be difficult to shift a culture that acts in silos and is slow to transform to one that experiments. After all, Peter Drucker, management consultant and author, believed large organisations could not be versatile as they are effective through their mass rather than agility. "Fleas can jump many times their own height, but not an elephant", he said. But large companies can take steps, starting with a small revolution that makes an incremental change to create a ripple effect and the success speaks for itself.

Many of the businesses we spoke to were encouraging a culture of experimentation and an intrapreneurial outlook. At the *Financial Times,* the approach to change was very much evolution rather than revolution. "It's continuous change and continuous learning and continuous evolution of what we do", says Fiona Spooner, who at the time of the interview in 2020 was the Global Marketing Director, B2C at the FT.

In this environment, in editorial, small teams were encouraged to come up with innovative ways of presenting the news.

Robin Kwong, who was the FT's head of digital delivery from 2017–19, spent his time trying to consider "new ways of storytelling or a new journalistic experience". He took the opportunity to learn about agile processes and applied those lessons to a newsroom context by creating news games or helping to develop other projects such as FT Globetrotter, a travel guide to cities on FT.com.

Anne Boden also leveraged her experiences from fintech and applied them to Allied Irish Banks, which she joined in 2012 as Chief Operating Officer before she went on to found challenger bank Starling. "I basically cleared out a whole floor . . . and said, this is where we're going to do the process reinvention", she says.

"We were very successful. We came up with processes, aiming for the best outcome from the start. We took the position that we could do it regardless of what challenges might lie ahead on the path to reinvention."

DEVELOP FAST AND GET FEEDBACK EARLY

Being unafraid of trying out new things is key for an organisation to keep moving forward. Minimum viable products (MVP), where a basic product or service is developed with sufficient features to entice early adopters, are a great way to get a new idea off the ground and generate feedback to improve it. An MVP can help to develop the offering past the initial development stage.

"They [MVPs] are not prototypes. They are the minimum level you can build or see or do that actually test the hypothesis that you are trying to prove", says Phil Neal, a digital transformation partner at Deloitte.

This can be a way that companies tackle the challenge of creating products.

FRAME YOUR QUESTIONS

You can take simple steps to initiate an MVP. First, come up with specific questions you want to answer and focus on value for customers and the business.

Deloitte works with its clients using an approach it calls 'Venture path', which helps structure and focus innovation effort, including MVPs.

"Some people think innovation is this creative thing, a black art, you need to sit in a darkened room and meditate", says Neal. "Beneath it, is a simple set of questions, business-led, where you learn or pivot on route or shutdown." You start by asking three key questions:

- Is there demand for this?
- Can we actually do it?
- Is it actually worth it?

"Only when you can answer yes to those three questions repeatedly as you work through the development of your thinking around innovation, are you on to a winner", says Neal.

This type of MVP approach was taken by Robin Kwong, who was the then Head of Digital Delivery in the FT newsroom in 2019. He was collaborating on a project to build a news game called 'The Trade-off', as part of a series of articles on the company of the future, which started life as a simple Google spreadsheet. The questions he was trying to answer were:

- Is the game an enjoyable and comprehensible experience?
- Can you actually get through it?
- Do you learn something out of it?

The team then ran small-scale user tests on "the most minimal version of what this game would be". With user testing, they were able to fix problems fast and make changes "quickly and quite cheaply" and build up the prototype from there, Kwong says.

The pandemic prompted many businesses to act fast. One sector that adapted swiftly was education, with universities, colleges and schools worldwide turning to virtual classes. The IE business school in Madrid was one of them and used the minimum viable product approach as a way to get webinars off the ground. IE did an "MVP external prototype with a small pile of classes", which were improved over the summer of 2020, says Jolanta Golanowska, Director of Learning Innovation at IE.

They rapidly went "beta in September" and collected feedback in October which led to further changes and another round of feedback. "It's just continuous improvement", she says.

FIONA SPOONER

Global Marketing Director, B2C, Financial Times (2017–21)

The marketing department at the FT took a minimum viable product approach to run a 'try before you buy' trial where consumers were given 30 days' free access to the website. After that time, they could move over to a slice of content or access for a smaller amount of money. "We built that as an MVP for testing with a goal to sell people on to something afterwards", says Fiona Spooner.

While it was well intentioned, the consensus was that the project "did not work because it cannibalised subscriptions", she says. They took steps to shut the project down quickly but at the same time they needed to encourage teams to be confident in experimentation.

But Spooner urges caution where the zeitgeist is to embrace failure. "There was a flurry of emails, saying: 'Isn't it great. This has failed'", she says. "I was like: No, it hasn't failed. It depends on what your mark of failure is. Yes, it hasn't made us loads of money. But, if you wrote it down with everyone in the room and said: 'Well, actually, we've learned that we can build this, this quickly, we've learned that we can set this live within a week.'"

The team had learnt that tens of thousands of people had signed up to the product and engaged with it. "There are all these things that did work. It's just we hadn't got the end of it right . . . but 70 per cent of that worked. Because people are encouraged to celebrate failure, it's almost easier to sell it as failed. Move on to the next."

HOW TO KEEP THE COST OF INNOVATION DOWN

In terms of using simple small-scale tests, Neal makes the point that you can innovate for £50 even in a big corporation by simply asking some customers if they would be interested in this product if we were to do it.

"You could stand the website up with a link that goes to a blank landing page, say if you were a chocolate bar manufacturer, and ask if you are interested in having a personalised choc bar, and then count how many clicks you get on that link", Neal says.

Then you could look at how you would technically do that with your supply chains. "You can start to do small low-cost pilots that get you to a point of confidence where you answer yes to all those questions before you go and ask for a bit more money before you do the next bit of hypothesis testing against each of those questions", he says.

This might be paid marketing or social media marketing to test demand in a more accurate way. Then you might look at the detail of how you would do it, and you might get into the business case. "Innovate around a business problem and have a simple structured approach that takes you through that cycle of innovation", he says. "Innovation is not hard, you just need to be hanging it on a reason to change, be that business value, citizen value or avoidance of known pain points in some capacity."

EXERCISE

Consider Deloitte's three key questions for a minimum viable product and write down your answers:

1. **Is there demand for this?** *Is there a customer wanting to pay for it? Have you validated real interest via, for example, surveys, benchmarking, trends? Is it solving a pain point such as at the Lawn Tennis Association where they could not serve as many customers as quickly they would like?*

2. **Can we actually do it?** *This is the question that many people start with innovation, usually driven out of a tech function. But it "is the wrong place" to begin, says Neal. "It is a solution looking for a problem." But it is one of several questions that should be asked. Do we have the budget, capacity, experience and the resources required at hand or do we have to look for outside help?*

   If you can answer yes to both of the above questions, you should then ask:

3. **Is it actually worth it?** *Can you do that cost-effectively and is the cost of doing it less than the pain point you are solving or the increment of business value you are delivering to the customer? Can we make forecasts (optimistic, realistic and/or pessimistic) of when we break even and then make a profit?*

   And we can add:

4. **What would be the simplest, fastest and easiest way to obtain answers to the questions above?** *(See the chocolate bar example above.) How can we engage with potential customers to obtain answers to our questions and hypotheses?*

You can talk about these questions with your team to gather different perspectives. This can be done at any stage, but preferably the earlier the better.

To go deeper into the methodologies, record your thoughts on the following questions:

- *How can you reduce waste and increase efficiency?*
- *What value are you creating for the customer and is it enough?*
- *How are you measuring progress and performance?*
- *What do you see that demonstrates that the teams are collaborating and communicating effectively?*

Either revisit your answers regularly or when you reach project milestones. They will not only help you to apply learnings at each stage and reflect on your next steps but also enable you to be proactive by giving you insights that you can lobby stakeholders with as your project develops.

It can become an 'innovation diary' so that you can build your case study and replicate change for other projects. We often get things done, but do not record how we did it. This will help you to work in a more conscious way for current and future projects.

OPEN UP TO INNOVATION

Companies are opening up the innovation process so that they can collaborate with experts and creatives externally, using their ideas, skills and technology to help drive their businesses forward.

One way they are doing this is through 'open innovation' where more traditional legacy companies share problems with start-ups for them to solve them in a more agile way, with different perspectives. As a leader, you can also take several steps to help your team open up to innovation:

- Build expertise in your team.
- Aim to become a leader who proactively develops networks to know who to connect with whom when a project comes up.
- If your company has an innovation hub, seek out who to connect with to see if your team can get involved and collaborate to seed and grow ideas.
- Facilitate interaction across departments: collaborate and cultivate professional networks and share ideas. Link up with other teams to exchange knowledge and views in team briefings to ensure creative and critical thinking.
- Build cross-industry relationships to widen your knowledge and hear other diverse perspectives and views.

If a company can carve out space for experimentation and flexibility, with no expectation of any particular result and no performance measurements, what may seem like a crazy idea could turn out to be a sustainable business project. Some set up a separate venturing unit that is insulated from some of the constraints of the core business. Otherwise, it would risk being killed off because it would look too different.

Deloitte typically finds that most of its clients are streamlining their businesses, with a few trying to enhance their operating models and channels, and only 10 per cent really trying to disrupt any given sector and looking at how to do things fundamentally different.

Among those groups, companies are also setting up innovation hubs. Sometimes, they will establish them with ring-fenced funding that needs to be protected and metered out in a different way to conventional projects where you submit a well-defined business case and plan with predictable outcomes at specific stages.

"They are trying to make today's business better. They are trying to expand a little bit, but not too far from the core of what they do today to avoid alienating their leaders and workforce, and so as not to need too much [that is] different by way of metrics and funding mechanisms, or business case development", Neal says.

Global insurer Mapfre, law firm Hogan Lovells and Nikkei, the owner of the *Financial Times,* have also all set up innovation hubs and they all aim to seed and grow ideas within their companies.

As part of Mapfre's open innovation policy, the insurer established Insur_space to develop products for younger consumers and to pique their interest in insurance. Two years later, it had collaborated with nearly 40 start-ups, on projects ranging from parametric insurance and agricultural risks to partnership investment on some venture capital funds, and had grown to become a global fast-track-to-market programme (see box on page 53).

Hogan Lovells, meanwhile, created a section called HL Solutions for innovation as part of an agile approach to developing its business. HL Solutions developed a consulting business so the company could "see how it was growing", says Michael Davison, Deputy Chief Executive Officer. "We had all sorts of interesting incubator-type projects in there", he says.

But you need to have a plan to fold the successful projects back into the business to prevent silos forming. "Once we got these things up and running, we put it back into the practice", he says.

At the FT, in partnership with its parent media company Nikkei Inc, a growth fund was launched in 2019 that provides up to £2 million annually to support entrepreneurial innovations and ventures, especially aimed at driving long-term quality subscriber engagement in the US market. *Tech Scroll Asia,* a weekly newsletter on technology trends, was the first initiative from this fund, to help boost readership.

Also at Nikkei in Tokyo, an AI laboratory was set up to create a space to think about future innovation. The Japanese media group also used external parties and start-ups to develop ideas such as AI video news where articles are summarised from text to voice automatically and read out by animated characters.

"We keep on developing new services and content which feeds to the tech transformation", says Taihei Shigemori, Manager of Nikkei's digital transformation department.

For large, traditional companies, especially in Japan, innovation "will not always be realised by one person or one divided department", he says. "If we want to do something new, and make it grow at a large scale, we have to connect several people and several departments and orchestrate several new stakeholders inside the company to achieve and develop some innovative product or services."

But not everyone agrees with this hub approach. Daniel Hegarty, founder of online mortgage company, Habito, who saw his business triple in size over a period of 18 months, is cautious about using separate units: "The second you put innovation in a separate building, or on a different floor of the office, you are making it a very literal statement that the rest of the business isn't innovative; you're fostering an 'I only innovate over here' mentality and culture. You have to find a way to get shorter decision-making and experimental cycles to exist at the core of your company and that requires some incredible bravery."

This goes back to the importance of constant iteration in executing successful innovation processes. It is also important to consider if you can manage the innovation process yourself or if you need the help of external partners as in the case of Mapfre.

PABLO FERNANDEZ IGLESIAS

Head of Business Development and Innovation at Mapfre Assistance

Global insurer Mapfre set up an innovation hub because "it is no secret that the insurance industry is not the most innovative in the world", says Pablo Fernandez Iglesias.

"We realised we needed to have a separate core dedicated to deal with innovation" so it could be brought into the business itself, leveraging the company's international capabilities, he says.

▶

The hub covers three main areas: strategic/incremental, disruptive/exponential innovation and mobility as a specific focus due to the importance of motor insurance for the company.

Under the brand name Insur_space by Mapfre, the insurer provides units whereby technological partners in different ecosystems can interact, enabling digital transformation. They can also connect with education centres, universities and business schools.

The hub helped the company to "understand the new realities, which could be integrated in our value proposition, enabling us to be relevant in the different ecosystems where insurance plays a role", says Fernandez.

"Having an open innovation platform within the company enabled us to understand better what was going on outside and to filter those innovations that we can find in the digital environment and adapt them to the needs of our business. And not only for today, but also for the future."

This helps Mapfre to be competitive in a market where even big tech such as Amazon and Alibaba are interested in insurance. These global technology groups are redefining the customer digital experience and service automation and the insurance industry needs to understand what that means, says Fernandez.

What Mapfre tries to do is to make people aware that insurance provides value to them. One way of doing this is leveraging services, not only on the traditional insurance cover, but on all those services related to insurance. For example, a digital health insurance platform also provides customers with other lifestyle-related services "so we need to understand how we can leverage on services to make customers perceive the value of what an insurance company can give", he says.

By working on innovation projects and talking to start-ups, Mapfre increased knowledge of the insurance industry in the wider fintech community. This in turn drove cultural change within the organisation by developing the talent they had internally, creating intrapreneurs, as well as bringing tech talent into the workplace to build a case for innovation.

"We have developed the talent of the people we had, and we have been able to access external talent . . . and make them work together", says Fernandez.

EXPECT THE UNEXPECTED

Part of leading transformation is being able to adapt to unexpected outcomes from projects you may be running. You will need to prepare and be able to act on negative or positive results. What you can do:

- Minimise the cost of the project so that you limit any fallout if it fails, using MVPs.
- Be flexible so you can respond quickly to surprising results by having a Plan B.
- Learn and move on by applying discoveries into the next projects.

Mapfre, for example, benefited from creating an entrepreneurial spirit in the company and improving the understanding of internal stakeholders who recognised the value the hub brought them as well as increasing the speed of innovation. This was seen during the pandemic in particular when clients began demanding new products or services, such as multi-channel access to digital health, lifestyle or home assistance solutions.

The response from Mapfre teams was seen in the "agility to implement" changes at a rapid pace. "They went far beyond what was expected from them, integrating themselves in other teams in order to provide customer support, interacting with technology to make sure that we were able to deliver in a shorter timeframe. So our teams really surprised us", says Fernandez.

For legacy firms, they can attract more relevant talent by making their innovation approach visible to external stakeholders through publicity and open challenges.

This is especially important in the fintech sector as it becomes more software-focused. New tech profiles, such as data, cybersecurity and digital marketing experts, will also need to be incorporated for those companies to stay relevant, where agile incumbents are stealing market share.

NNEILE NKHOLISE

Co-founder of 3D-IMO

3D-IMO is a South African start-up that automates livestock data analytics. When Nneile Nkholise was looking into the early detection of viral infections in animals, her investigations turned up some unexpected results that took her business in a different direction.

▶

Her company had been investigating using infrared images to pick up heat signatures in animals because there was an increasing problem in South Africa with cattle dying from preventable diseases, either through lack of vaccination or failure to detect the risk of viral infection. So when a cow has a high temperature, the idea was the photo, using backend artificial intelligence, could help denote a disease risk.

But they faced a challenge. "We could not identify the cattle that we were working with. So we were literally taking a picture or video of a cattle but we did not have identification of that cattle", says Nkholise, who was recognised in the top 100 young Africans by the Africa Youth Council in 2018.

This led to an unexpected discovery that the cows could be identified by using their muzzle because its pattern – the wrinkles on their noses – is as unique as a human fingerprint and you can use it to carry out biometric identification. "We can also print out QR codes that can be attached to a tag of an animal", she says.

This meant that this method could help farmers identify their animals where previously they had struggled to do so because it was very labour-intensive for small holders.

"With our technology, we started to generate ownership so when you created a biometric identification it links an animal to a farmer. So wherever the cow is you can take a picture of it and it will tell you who the owner is. This then led to a further unexpected outcome. The information could also be used to build up data insights for the farmers and give them an indication of how their farm was performing. "We started helping farmers how to build data insights for them to be able to focus on farming and not on the admin that takes so much time", she says.

Not only that, she is able to use that data to build partnerships with banks and insurance companies, which at times found it difficult to provide cover to livestock farmers because they did not have insights on disease risk or even ownership.

Cattle farmers pose a security risk to banks, which have been reluctant to provide credit solutions because livestock moves around easily, she says. "You would find a farmer who would say he had 200 cattle and when a banker goes to look at the cattle, they would see 200. But the farmer only has 40 cattle and the other 160 they borrowed from neighbouring farms. So it has always been such a difficult challenge for banks."

In 2018, Nkholise made one of the most coveted lists, Forbes Africa 30 under 30.

WHAT DO YOU STOP DOING?

Organisations may say they embrace failure, but when it comes to it, they find that difficult to do. Looking at ways to experiment can be harder than it appears because you will need to realise when a project is failing and close it down quickly when something is not working. If you are failing too long, with your project lingering and dying a slow death, the problem is you are not achieving what you set out to do. This wastes time, resources and money.

"It is much harder to stop something than start it because you get some kind of proudness into it", says Trond Sundnes, of his time leading a digital transformation project internally at Norway's largest business newspaper, *Dagens Naeringsliv* (see box Page 59).

If a project is failing and it needs to be closed down, typical warning signs can include:

- **A loss of focus:** You may even no longer know why you are continuing to run with a project.
- **Consistently not reaching milestones:** Stakeholders start to lose interest in the project as the project becomes mired in delays.
- **Failure to review:** Feedback and monitoring progress may have tailed off.
- **Loss of budget:** Other projects are being funded and not yours.
- **Loss of resources:** Staff who leave are not being replaced.
- **Loss of project leader:** They have moved on and no one has replaced them.

Michael Davison, Deputy Chief Executive at Hogan Lovells, who was due in 2021 to look at which projects to wind down at the firm, agrees it is hard to shut projects: "We did not fail quickly." It is "psychological" because "it becomes their baby" and people do not want to part company with the project.

You may have heard of the mantra 'fail fast, fail often'. But what is actually meant by that is learning from your mistakes and using short cycles to improve.

In the start-up world, especially in the US, investors often say that they are not interested in founders who have not previously failed. They do this because when we fail we are more conscious of what we have to change to succeed.

WHEN DO YOU SHUT IT DOWN?

You need to be realistic and ask a simple set of questions at various stages of your project and shut it down if it is not passing these tests. They can include:

- **What is working?** Check what is successful and what is not and if progress is acceptable or more negative than positive according to objectives. If outcomes are proving to be continuously more negative than positive over the planned time line, it is a sign to close the project down.
- **What can be improved?** Obtain feedback from all stakeholders to help you decide what improvements or adjustments, if any, can be made.
- **What are the obstacles?** What is taking up your time and using the most energy in a non-productive way? Are these hurdles surmountable?
- **What are the next steps?** Are they clear or do they have to be redefined?

Other points to consider include:

- How are you measuring whether you and your team meet the desired outcomes? What method or key performance indicators (KPIs) are you using?
- How much time have you set aside for the project? Is it enough? If you are stretched, maybe more time and/or resources have to be allocated. Can you afford to do this?
- How long are you taking to be creative? Creativity normally comes when we have space and time to think. Are you being more reactive rather than proactive?
- How will you monitor whether the idea can turn from investment to return? How will it generate a bottom line? Be careful here because it is not a one-size fits all. Have you discussed the business model and made a profit and loss forecast? How does the technical time line match this forecast and when must you start offering something that will generate income?

"Everyone says: 'Embrace failure'", Neal says. "We don't mean embrace failure where you drop £15 million on something that was a non-starter from day one. We mean do simple empirical tests at various stages of commitment on a simple set of commercial questions and use that to pivot or shut down what you are doing – throughout you adopt a deliberate and metered approach to funding."

Michael Davison, Deputy Chief Executive Officer who drives digital strategy at law firm Hogan Lovells, agrees with ending a project sooner rather than later: "Act decisively and quickly and fail quickly. Companies can be so scared of failing and they tend to overplan and overthink and then become very reluctant to pull the plug.

"The bigger the organisation, the bigger the temptation to overplan. You can have great ideas but you can overthink them. You need to act on the lightbulb moment, just do it rather than let it fade. Have a dynamic environment. If it takes six months to plan and implement, life has moved on."

But Michelle Senecal de Fonseca, who has run the sales and services organisation for Citrix, cautions against creating a 'fear culture' around innovation: "Nobody knows how this is going to work and you are going to make mistakes and that is OK. You just need to call it experimentation."

"As long as you can make sure you manage the risk, people should be allowed to say, 'OK that didn't work that well so let's try what we need to do next'. People have to want to put themselves in that situation."

In the new world of work, managers have to be comfortable with trial and error, she says. "A lot of our management practices from previous decades have been about maintaining control and command. We place such a high value on winning that control is paramount and there isn't an acceptance of loss. In that environment, people don't willingly take on much risk.

"That's not what the new world is about. Markets, technology, competition are all moving too quickly and few have the knowledge or historical trends to know how old-world control should be applied. You need to move towards agile experimentation where you can safely try, adapt and deploy."

TROND SUNDNES

Chief Executive Officer at NHST Global Publications and former Development Editor at Dagens Naeringsliv (DN), the Norwegian business news organisation

Trond Sundnes had a target of six months to make a daily business news website a viable product but as the deadline loomed, he and his team were not even close to making it happen. But it proved difficult to close down and despite missing the targets, it limped on. "We couldn't end it", he says.

▶

Initially, the project got off to a flying start as DN's response to US media company BuzzFeed increased its audience share at the time. It was 2015 and senior managers believed the model should be based around advertising and sponsorship, rather than subscriptions (such as that at the Financial Times) to raise revenue.

"Within three months we had made a web page, we were ready", Sundnes says, but it only took about six weeks before he was embroiled in an internal struggle over headcount. You could have the argument over resources every single day, he says, as there was "always something more important happening" in the newsroom.

Over time, fewer stories were being published as staff were redeployed elsewhere. When the plug was finally pulled, it was big news in Norway – with a lot of negative feedback. "We got readers saying I want to leave DN and quit my subscription", says Sundnes. "We should have [stopped the project] earlier."

Without that experiment, though, many things "would not have happened later" because he and his colleagues had learnt a lot.

Having to end a project should not stop you from trying out other ideas. "Don't be afraid of doing new things", he says. If he were to run something similar again, he would set up a team with dedicated staff to run it. "Ensure they have one mission to do. That would be my ideal. And have a short period of six months to ensure we get it."

When they went on to establish another website, they used the same design and just changed some colours and logo. "We learnt how to do things faster. We knew that we had to set targets", he says. "The first half year after [the business news website] disaster I tried not to speak about it. After a year, I actually took it up and showed it to everyone. I explained: remember this disaster, it actually got us here."

SPEED AND SCALE

The upheaval of the pandemic led many companies to speed up their digital strategies, accelerating change that usually takes a few years to months. They saw "two years' worth of digital transformation in two months", says Satya Nadella, Microsoft's Chief Executive, in a Financial Times article.

Both Microsoft and Amazon, which run the two biggest cloud platforms, saw their stock market values propelled above $1.5 trillion that year on hopes that it pointed to a lasting shift. According to a McKinsey Global survey of executives, companies increased the pace of digitisation of customer and supply-chain interactions and of their internal operations by three to four years. The share of digital or digitally enabled products in their portfolios has accelerated by seven years, it said. Nearly all respondents said their companies met many of the new demands more quickly than they had thought possible before the crisis. Respondents expect most of these changes to be long-lasting and are already making the kinds of investments that all but ensure they will stick.

"The whole world shifted to ecommerce overnight – most companies weren't ready for that", Jennifer Tejada, Chief Executive of PagerDuty, which sells an incident response service used by corporate IT departments, told the FT in July 2020. As a result, "things we thought were going to take years got pulled forward to this year and done in months".

Connie Nam of Astrid & Miyu, which saw its sales grow by 1,000 per cent in three years to 2021, pivoted quickly to holding digital styling consultations as physical stores shut. "We couldn't really do that personalised service" because the shops had closed, she says, but, "having the human touch with customers and really engaging" with them was important so her company replicated that experience digitally.

They tailored the content and initially "weren't trying to sell". They were communicating messages such as self-care. "That really resonated with our customers, and they naturally came on to our website. So I would say during the first lockdown, our online sales grew at 150 per cent year on year."

Zoom Video Communications also scaled at a "startlingly incredible clip", says Abe Smith, Head of International. "We saw every metric just go through the roof in terms of free user and paid user accounts." The business was able to demonstrate it could architecturally scale and the software was "extremely advanced" and capable of effectively expanding infinitely, he says.

The online video-conferencing business went from 1.2 billion to over 3 trillion meeting minutes per year consumptions, from 10 million daily participants to over 300 million meeting participants. And that happened in about seven months.

"It put a tremendous stress on our employees on other functions [such as customer service] . . . the systems were not built for that kind of consumption." Security concerns became an issue that Zoom had to "focus on ardently". But "one of the benefits was that the company is extremely agile. We were adaptive. We listened to the market".

"When you are in the middle of the epicentre it's fight or flight. You had to step up. It was everybody grab a mop and let's go clean. Let's work together and that really showed the fortitude of the company and it also showed what's possible."

WHAT TO DO NEXT

1. Reflect on how you may be able to apply a mix of the three methods in your workplace.

2. Monitor progress to check if goals are being met, being open to unexpected results.

3. Have the strength and courage to stop doing something if it is not working and regroup. But scale what is working.

FURTHER READING

Coaching Agile Teams: A Companion for ScrumMasters, Agile Coaches, and Project Managers in Transition by Lyssa Adkins

The Toyota Way by Jeffrey K Liker

The Lean Start-up by Eric Ries

Thinking, Fast and Slow by Daniel Kahneman

Scrum Mastery by Jeff Cohn

Making Work Visible by Dominica Degrandis

The FT's trade-off game: https://ig.ft.com/esg-purpose-profit-game/

More on Robin Kwong's experience of developing the game: https://source.opennews.org/articles/how-we-used-google-sheets-newsgame-prototype/

CHAPTER 4

THE HUMAN TOUCH: WHAT MACHINES CAN'T DO

Digital transformation is *"100 per cent soft skills"*, says Anastasia Leng, co-founder of CreativeX, and they will continue to be in high demand as the pace of automation accelerates in the workplace.

We have found in our and others' experience that the human side – managing and leading people – has been the critical make or break factor in change projects.

Here we will take you through the key soft skills that will help you prepare and support colleagues and build winning teams. These include:

- *Understanding your team.*

- *Adding the extra ingredient that can make the difference between success and failure, turning good into exceptional.*

- *Building trust.*

- *Being able to influence and persuade.*

- *Looking after yourself.*

WHAT WILL MAKE YOU STAND OUT AS A LEADER

As the use of artificial intelligence grows, so will the need for emotional intelligence – the ability to be aware of, express and control one's emotions and to understand the feelings of others and handle them appropriately. This is what will make leaders stand apart from machines as collaboration rather than competition within organisations is going to be key during an era where many tasks will be automated.

Being able to deal with people effectively, as well as solve problems and develop a 'growth' mindset, where you can rise to challenges and learn from mistakes, will also continue to be valued.

"It is in the softer areas of resource management that leaders may need to pay the most attention", said a report by Headspring, an executive development joint venture with the *Financial Times* and IE business school in Spain. "In the years to come, companies in which people collaborate best will have a competitive edge, and to that extent emotional intelligence will be more vital", according to a summary of Daniel Goleman's book *Working with Emotional Intelligence*. If the human ingredient is ignored, Goleman warned, nothing else will work as well as it might.

Meri Williams, former Chief Technology Officer at Monzo, agrees: "The emotional journey matters more than the rational side of things. Change is an emotional process and forgetting about the human side is the fastest way to guarantee failure."

She has overseen many digital transformation projects in her career in the technology sector, ranging from the UK government and retailer Marks and Spencer to challenger bank Monzo and online print and design company Moo. "A relatively small set of people are convinced by logic and explanation or data. For everybody else, you need something aspirational – a picture of the future that is inspiring", she says.

UNDERSTAND YOUR TEAM

Whether you are asked to put together a team for a transformation project, or you inherit a department, it is important to understand what skill sets you need or have. Talent management and the way we work is transforming rapidly. At top business schools much attention is paid to how to lead diverse groups to optimum performance.

You should start by assessing the strengths and gaps in skills in the team and also be open to redefining roles to recruit wider, more varied perspectives. We will go into more detail about what steps you can take to increase diversity in your workplace in Chapter 6.

To deepen understanding of what the team does well, you can use a type of strengths finder such as the one developed by researcher and management consultant Meredith Belbin. His model looks at how people behave in the workplace and which roles best suit them and it is widely used across many sectors.

Belbin looks at team versus individual performance. When you are assigned to do something by yourself, you will do it. But when you work as a team, you can balance each other by working on your strengths, if you are aware of what they are.

His approach has been deployed by many companies to build the right and most effective teams by harnessing strengths and containing weaknesses. Belbin's method can also help you to identify who is best for each role and how people can be put together in a team to take on a challenge. "We should concentrate on the role we play best and that way we show ourselves to advantage. If we try to play every role, we will end up undermining the role other people will play", Belbin says in a YouTube video.

He identified nine team roles, which are defined as a tendency to behave, contribute and interrelate in a certain way, and put them into three groups:

action, people and thought-oriented. Individuals can take on two or more of these roles in any given team.

The roles have strengths and 'allowable' weaknesses, in that you can improve on them once you are aware of them. They include two possible leaders, one expert and one ideas person – the innovator. All the others are either doers, such as implementers or evaluators, or people who communicate and give support.

According to the website www.Belbin.com, the roles are made up of the following.

Group	Role	Strengths	Allowable weaknesses	Don't be surprised to find . . .	Who is this in your team?
Action	Shaper	Dynamic. Overcomes obstacles	May offend people's feelings	Risk becoming aggressive to get things done	
	Implementer	Practical and reliable. Turns ideas into action	Can be inflexible	Slow to relinquish their plans in favour of positive changes	
	Completer Finisher	Most effectively used at the end of tasks. Perfects and polishes	Reluctant to delegate	Could take perfectionism to extreme	
People					
	Co-ordinator	Draws out team's objectives. Clarifies goals. Identifies talent	Can offload their work	Might over-delegate	
	Team worker	Helps team to gel. Listens and averts friction. Diplomatic	Tends to avoid confrontation	Hesitant to make unpopular decisions	

Group	Role	Strengths	Allowable weaknesses	Don't be surprised to find . . .	Who is this in your team?
	Resource investigator	Explores opportunities and develops contacts. Outgoing	Over-optimistic. Can lose interest after initial enthusiasm	May forget to follow up on lead	
Thought					
	Plant	Creative, imaginative, free-thinking, generates ideas and solves difficult problems	Might ignore incidentals. Too preoccupied to communicate effectively	Can be forgetful	
	Monitor-evaluator	Strategic, logical and discerning	Lacks the drive and ability to inspire others	Slow at decision-making	
	Specialist	Single-minded, self-starting and dedicated	Tends to contribute on narrow front	Can overload you with information	

EXERCISE

Belbin also shows that any project has four key steps:

1. *Initiation (start)*

2. *Creation (brainstorming)*

3. *Implementation (application and making)*

4. *Completion (finishing within deadlines)*

▶

This is an exercise you can do by yourself to understand your strengths or preferences, or in a team setting of up to ten members. If you go for the team option, you must give equal support to each member, without any judgement.

If you feel you are not able to do this, it may be worth finding out if your workplace would provide and fund a professional trainer or facilitator to help you.

- Draw a circle that has four equally sized quadrants with the words Initiation, Creation, Implementation and Completion in a clockwise order.

- Place the circle in front of yourself and/or your team. If you are doing it on your own, choose two quadrants where you would prefer to be according to your strengths and motivation. Otherwise, ask each team member to choose two quadrants for themselves. Belbin comments that we can normally only feel strong in two areas.

- Everyone taking part in this should think about this for five minutes and then add their initials to two quadrants.

- Next, if you are doing this on your own, reflect on your findings. Otherwise discuss as a team to see if, as a group, everyone is working to their strengths and preferences.

If a quadrant is empty or has only a few initials, the team can consider how to compensate and fill those gaps. For example, if they have no people in 'Creation' they could hold an event where they meet to brainstorm options.

By using this technique, you should be able to have a structured conversation with your team to help them see if they are working in a way that motivates them and to their best capabilities. It should generate the sharing of information which could be acted on.

HOW TO BUILD AN INNOVATION BASE – INTRINSIC MOTIVATION

Once you have understood your team, you can look at what motivates them to perform, become highly driven and innovate. Here, the soft skills are as essential as the 'hard' or technical abilities. The human factor is that extra ingredient, which is needed in a difficult and challenging environment.

Daniel Pink, author of best-selling books about business, work and behaviour, has identified when people give you that bit more – that 'discretionary effort'. In his book *Drive*, he calls this the intrinsic motivation. If you can get people to work because they want to do it, or they feel proud about it, they will give more "for free".

For intrinsic motivation to work, though, you also need external factors, identified by US psychologist Abraham Maslow as, for example, having enough cash to pay the rent and adequate working conditions.

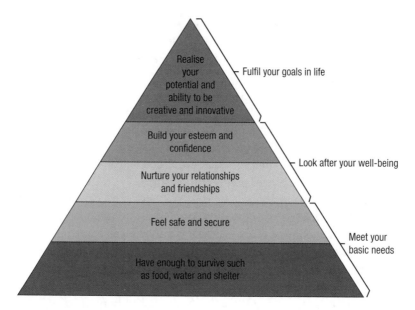

Figure 4.1 Hierarchy of needs
Based on Maslow's Hierarchy of Needs.

Maslow created a hierarchy of needs, as shown in the triangle, and said you cannot go higher up if the needs at each level are not covered. They are the 'hygiene factors'.

If we cover the basic needs as well as psychological ones, such as a feeling of accomplishment, we can achieve our maximum potential, be creative and add value. This is the ideal context to drive change and innovation. By creating the right environment, you might get more effort back without having to incentivise financially.

Pink identifies the following to make people go the extra mile:

- **Purpose:** Understand the meaning of the project for each team member.
- **Autonomy:** Give people autonomy to tackle tasks as they see fit to validate their experience and expertise.
- **Mastery:** Let them learn while they are working.

If we can create this context, it is more likely that team members will make an additional 'discretionary' extra effort because the context is positive and supportive.

You can apply it be doing the following three actions.

1 FIND A PURPOSE

Once you have enough money, it will not necessarily make you more creative but if your manager gives you a sense of purpose, where you feel you are doing something good for yourself and others, you are likely to give more to it. An aspect of this might be where employees can pursue personal goals in a work environment.

When Frank De Winne was in command of the ISS every person had some individual goals. "Some people may want to take a lot of pictures of the earth. Others want to make videos for education, like I was doing. These are some personal goals that you also have to accommodate and see how we can fit these in the overall goal of the mission."

In Japan, having a purpose in life is called 'ikigai'. This concept can be used to define your career goals, including what you are good at, what you need to do and what you are passionate about. If team members can work to their strengths, understand the requirements of the project and be motivated, change management is more likely to succeed.

2 'STAND IN SOMEONE ELSE'S SHOES BUT KEEP YOUR SOCKS ON'

Autonomy is also important for a skilled worker. If you tell people what to do and you are in a position of power they are probably going to do it. But if you give them a sense of value and ask them how they would like to do it you are more likely to get a long-term positive response.

Seeing transformation from someone else's perspective is a powerful tool and one that managers can put into practice.

Andy Pierce, who at the time of the interview was Editorial Product Manager for NHST Global Publications, saw the benefit of this when he was having to introduce a transformation project: "There was a nice phrase from our head of HR: how do you stand in someone else's shoes but keep your own socks on?"

At his workplace, during the pandemic in 2020 a peer group of managers was created across the Norwegian business news organisation DN and Global Publications. And they were given regular training on everything from management to change in a crisis. "Creating this management group created something that didn't exist before to help with the soft skills", says Pierce.

The way Michelle Senecal de Fonseca tries to see it from another perspective at Citrix is to take on her managerial reportees' roles when they become vacant. This gives her the opportunity to get her 'hands dirty' so she can understand the challenges the team faces and what they can do to deal with them. "In the old world, you became a manager because you developed into being the best at something and your role was to teach others to do it well too", she says. "Yet as a leader, you may not even understand all elements of your team's work but what you need to focus on is inspiring them to want to do their best work and align to common goals and purposes.

"If you show you are willing to occasionally get into the trenches to understand the challenges they face and the complexities of their roles" you are more likely to gain their trust and commitment to the larger goals.

ABE SMITH

Head of International, Zoom Video Communications, US video-conferencing company

Soft skills are the centre of core values for Zoom, from employees to customers and the wider community. And they are summed up in one word: happiness. By keeping employees happy, thereby activating their intrinsic motivation as Daniel Pink says, staff will give more and work better.

"Culture is extremely important at Zoom and the company is focused around our core value of delivering happiness to employees, customers and our communities", says Abe Smith.

In 2019 and 2020 Zoom was the top company with the happiest employees, according to anonymous employee feedback to Comparably.com, a website covering company cultures. The business even has a team – a happiness crew – to provide contentment not only to employees but to the community and outreach as well. "The core mission for the company was to ensure that we did the right thing", says Smith.

In fact, when Zoom was set up in 2011, the thesis for the company was built around the fact that "people were disappointed" with the products available at that time as they were not designed for the modern worker, he said. The market had evolved but the services had not.

▶

"There was a fundamental belief in collaboration and an understanding that the way people use video would be, or could be, disrupted, specifically given the fact that the then present solutions weren't solving what people needed."

Zoom was tested in the pandemic, when at the start of 2020, the company had roughly 10 million meeting participants every day and by March that usage went up to 200 million and a month later Zoom was somewhat of a household name with over 300 million participants daily, from governments and schools to small business owners and sole traders.

"We were principled correctly", says Smith, but the success "goes back to the core values and the mission of the company. We realised this was our calling."

"We realised we had a responsibility to the world and we led with the concept that we will figure everything out but right now focus on helping the world whether that is students maintaining educational continuity or governments being able to govern and communicate with constituents."

During the pandemic, Zoom had faced challenges from rapid growth, especially after a spate of security and privacy lapses. Those issues have been fixed, the company has said. The business is 'hyper transparent'.

"I'd say trust is associated with transparency and . . . we place a lot of trust and responsibility on employees who are new to the company, industry or the role", says Smith. "Generally speaking, we are pleasantly surprised to see what happens when you lend your trust to people."

3 ALWAYS LEARNING

With mastery, learning on the job is an extra bonus that enhances the way you work. If you feel you have some freedom or are being trained, you are likely to feel more satisfied and be able to deal with innovation, which is becoming more unpredictable because the cycles are shorter and changing rapidly.

With a change management programme, you typically need to roll out some sort of training or re-skilling initiative so that the workforce can adapt to the new environment and reduce their anxieties around their roles.

Training is something that Senecal de Fonseca encourages at Citrix. "You constantly have to be learning and you have to be willing to do it yourself and your team needs to see it", she says. "They also have to have that same hunger because that is the only way we are going to move forward."

At the FT, training was ongoing where learning new skills was integrated into editorial as a matter of course. This helped to increase confidence among the workforce in adapting to'a newsroom facing perpetual change. What is more, sometimes with digital transformation projects, they have never been done before.

There is no blueprint to follow. And the technology may not even have been invented yet. This was the case at Spanish utility Iberdrola where as part of its 11-year project to deliver smart meters to its Spanish customers, it had to work out what technology it was going to need to help it succeed and develop it.

"That was part of the exhilarating feeling of being part of creating something that does not exist", says Nico Arcauz. "It was challenging but it was extremely rewarding for all of us who took part in that."

WHY TRUST IS KEY

Trust is one of the most transversal themes in innovation. It is about believing that something is good, honest, safe and reliable. We believe this is the number one key skill that managers need to deliver successful projects. Many of the leaders we interviewed said the capacity to build trust was vital.

According to the 2020 Edelman Trust barometer report, people grant their trust on competence and ethical behaviour. And in 2018, the barometer showed that 70 per cent of the main job of a chief executive is to build trust.

"You demand trust that we'll all be working together to the vision", says Anne Boden, Chief Executive of Starling, a digital bank.

It is based on three things: empathy, authenticity and credibility. This is because people tend to trust you when they believe they are interacting with the real you (authenticity), Frances Frei and Anne Morriss wrote in *Harvard Business Review*. This develops faith in your judgment (logic/credibility), and when they feel you care about them (empathy).

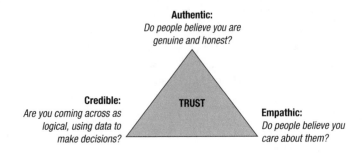

Figure 4.2 The trust triangle

Adapted from 'Begin and Trust' by Frances Frei and Anne Morriss, May-June 2020.

These three elements make up the trust triangle, which also contains groups: the leader's role in innovation, how the leader relates to employees, and finally, the customer.

As a manager you will need to be able to connect, understand, motivate and listen as well as be authentic for your team to feel you are being honest. You will also need logic, backed up by credible data.

"You have to be your authentic self", advises Abe Smith, Head of International at Zoom. "That's true for the company. Stick to your values. We lead with a north star and we believe in doing the right thing."

Trust is "massively important" in transformation and it "comes from the top" of the company, he says.

HOW THE TRUST TRIANGLE WORKS

The more likely you are to complete the trust triangle, the more you can affect the three groups and create something of value. To make it work, you are likely to have to look at what trust means for each person in your team. It could be as simple as arriving at a meeting on time or doing what you commit to or being honest and saying you cannot do something.

To dive deeper into these themes, look at the three factors that make the trust triangle:

- **Authenticity:** Ask yourself and a trusted peer if you are being clear and honest with yourself and the team. Do you need to do anything differently? (It is sometimes easier for others to see this rather than yourself.)
- **Empathy:** Ask yourself and a trusted peer if you are really connecting with your colleagues and seeing it from their perspective. Do you need to rethink any aspect of how you come across?

■ **Logic:** Are you backing up your statements and actions with credible, objective data? If not, look to add data into your team briefings and other workplace communication.

In order to build trust with colleagues, you will not only be having open conversations but also setting the same mission, whether you are an astronaut or a manager in a corporation.

If you ask an astronaut what capacities and values are necessary for a successful mission, the answer is likely to include various soft skills from collaboration and resilience to empathy and active listening. But one of the most important is trust. No wonder: when a rocket lifts off, the astronauts' lives quite literally depend on the work of thousands of strangers.

"You need to build trust with the Ground", says Frank De Winne, Belgian's second man in space as commander of the International Space Station in 2009. "On the Ground, you don't know all of them. You have a more remote connectivity. But it is important to be transparent and sometimes things go wrong."

And if things do go wrong, the astronauts need to talk through the next steps with Ground Control. "You cannot live six months in the space station and do 1,000 tasks per day and not have something that does not work, or fails or make a mistake", he says.

Building that up on the ISS is just the same as in a team in a corporation, where soft skills such as transparency and honesty are paramount to developing an effective group dynamic.

"Being honest with your crew mates" and "making sure everyone has the same information as you" was crucial, says De Winne.

At Iberdrola, Nico Arcauz agrees: "Be honest, never lie to people."

NICO ARCAUZ

Head of Smart Grids Global and Spain, Iberdrola, Spanish utility

Nico Arcauz says he thought like a psychologist while overseeing a project at Iberdrola that included inventing technology to roll out smart meters to 11 million customers across Spain.

Emotional intelligence was at the heart of his journey, as people from different cultures – and languages – were brought together to form an international team from across the business, which also operates in the UK, US and Brazil.

▶

He says he had to "manage the psychological aspect of the project. You are transforming the processes that are core to the business. You needed to manage the psychological response of the people involved because the whole organisation was involved."

He had to secure the buy-in of 4,000 employees. That was "a challenge and I have no easy answer for that", he says. "The first reaction of the people is that this is not for me . . . You need to manage those triggers to engage everyone on board, give training and give emotional support, be truthful. It is a mix of respect and trust and it works both ways. You have to understand differences exist but you need to live with it and you need to embrace it and understand the origin of that difference. At the same time you need to cooperate and make it work."

It also comes back to having the same goal or mission. "We are all in the same boat. We are all 100 per cent Iberdrola", he says. "We are different but we have to acknowledge it and we have to work together."

They broke down the execution into well-defined phases. The first one was a pilot of 1 per cent of the meter base – 100,000 customers. The second replicated the pilot in the four Spanish regions in which Iberdrola operates. The third scaled up to include all customers. This gradual approach helped to "manage the psychological feeling that you are trying to overcome the natural opposition of people where they apply the law of least effort and the law of not changing and being in their comfort zone", he says.

They also chose wisely where that first pilot operated. One of the criteria was selecting an area where "we knew we were going to receive a positive reaction from the people because they wanted to be frontrunners [and] they felt comfortable with something new", he says. If they had chosen managers who were "not so much prone to change or even opposed to change . . . the outcome would have been totally different".

After the first pilot was successful, the company benefited from a growing number of change champions. They now had "ten times the ambassadors that we had from the beginning" for the new technology.

His advice is to try to make changes gradually: "Put out fires as soon as you identify them and not add any fuel to the fire. Try to explain things from the very first day and manage those threats because people will feel threatened."

"Don't forget in order to be successful, people must enter the equation otherwise you will suffer", he says.

HOW TO INFLUENCE AND PERSUADE

Once you have established that people can trust you, you should be able to influence and persuade colleagues and inspire them to drive change.

Influence is how you affect others because of your way of being and your presence, what they know and think of you passively, while persuasion is based on techniques that are more intentional and active.

The Greek philosopher Aristotle summarised the importance of these two skills when he talked about ethos, logos and pathos:

- **Ethos** is 'You'. You need to have credibility, self-confidence, presence and authority as people tend to believe those they respect.

- **Logos** is the 'Message'. Explain the content and benefits of your message to your audience. It is the logic of why it should happen.

- **Pathos** is your 'Client. Have empathy and understand the drivers and needs of those you are addressing. They are then more likely to be influenced and persuaded.

Today, it is important to have the two skills in your leadership toolkit and you can develop them by doing a mix of the following:

- Use facts to support your arguments for transformation.

- Assert yourself by stating expectations and using incentives.

- Involve people, asking for their views and respecting their opinion.

- Listen, summarise their feelings and share a common vision.

You can refer back to Chapter 2 to read more about how to communicate effectively and why involving and supporting internal and external stakeholders is crucial. Your human capital and reputation can also affect this in both a positive and negative way, so looking after relationships at all levels is important, before and after your change project.

EXERCISE

Consider how you influence and persuade your team with the three elements of ethos, logos and pathos. Are you using those three elements for maximum effect?

Think about what ways you could enhance how you do this in your verbal and written messages.

MERI WILLIAMS

Former Head of Delivery at GDS, UK Government Digital Service

Cake and mascots were used by Meri Williams to break down silos when she inherited several multidisciplinary teams at GDS that "wouldn't talk to one another". She befriended someone from each team and asked them for input into what cake she would bake every week. "Every Monday morning, all these members knew I would be bringing baked goods in so they would all follow me into this tiny kitchen", she says. People who would not otherwise know each other built relationships in the queue – and that cake network can still be seen today.

If teams were very 'us and them', there were at least two people in the cake network who would be "shame-faced if I ended up having to come along and make them all talk nicely. Because they were at the cake thing, they couldn't be us and them . . . This informal network existed so that people saw each other as people and not as them", she says.

The teams were also asked to choose a mascot and Williams brought them a soft toy to represent them. When the teams were not talking, the toys would be invited to a meeting. "If two teams had been particularly aggro with each other I would put an invite in diaries and make the mascots of the teams attend. So it would be like the Griffin and the Badger are meeting next Tuesday and some humans should also probably attend", she says.

It was harder to argue with toys in the meeting and it boosted collaboration over time – as did setting the same goals across the teams.

During her time at GDS, she "started to bump up against the other organisations that needed to be involved" in the project. Gov.uk is an official communication channel of the government so security services were not only concerned about website breaches but whether someone could start a war. Her approach to win them over was to workshop the 'why' of what they were worried about, such as someone being employed who wanted to do the country harm and being able to push code directly from laptops into production.

"You are worried about someone being forced to do that and not being able to detect it at the time and you are also worried about things being accidentally published, such as pre-prepared documents", she says.

They came up with a compromise to only give the ability to deploy code to a few people who had passed a certain level of security clearance and seniority. They were also never allowed to deploy code alone. "With the security service, we tried to deeply understand what their concern was and then go well if we could come up with a way to prevent the thing you are worried about . . . would you entertain it. And they were willing to", she says.

"People are willing to flex if you flex to understand them. I think the change I brought was that previously there were just two sides very loudly restating what the right way to do it was. I got them to take three steps back and find out what they are worried about: they don't want to start a war."

WORKING TOGETHER

Once you are able to influence and persuade colleagues to help you drive transformation you can bring them together to collaborate. This is the other key skill that is necessary to drive change: working together in multidisciplinary teams creates the right environment for problem-solving and critical thinking.

"There is a sense of brainstorming and inclusion" in a transformation process, says Blathnaid Healy at CNN. In that long cycle that happens behind building, iterating and doing the lengthy transformation work, people at every level of the organisation must be engaged and collaborate, "otherwise it won't work", she says.

Along the way of building out a project you have to "learn to have honest conversations about what needs to happen, have the right tools to be able to figure those things out, have the right relationships around your organisation but ultimately making sure you've got the right people in the room doing the work and that you are listening to them", she says.

At CreativeX, the biggest signal that a partnership was likely to succeed was how good the other company was "at the softer side of things" when it came to change management. The start-up was asking businesses to digitally transform all the processes they had around video and imagery content and finding the right people to talk to was vital for the CreativeX team when they were trying to establish partnerships.

They had to work out whether a contact was someone "who is not just aware of the fact that rolling something like this out will require cross-functional, cross-national collaboration. It will require changing and supplementing existing processes. It will require multi-level stakeholder buy-in because we are talking about doing something that has simply not been done before", says Anastasia Leng.

LOOK AFTER YOURSELF

Leading transformation can be exhausting and change agents can be particularly at risk of burnout so building up your resilience to manage change is key. As the pace of change only accelerates, employees generally will need to be aware of any signs of stress, such as sleep problems, anxiety and consuming too much alcohol, to look after their well-being.

Particularly after the pandemic, companies are likely to have to spend a lot more time on the mental health of their employees.

In January 2020, a Deloitte report on mental health and employers found that the costs to UK employers of poor mental health was £45 billion.

There has been a shift over the past ten years to provide support for staff after high-profile cases such as Antonio Horta-Osario, the then Lloyds bank Chief Executive, took a leave of absence in 2011 after suffering from stress-induced insomnia. That experience led him to review support for the bank's 65,000 employees and introduce a number of measures including mental health officers.

Citrix has also trained up mental health first aiders. "People can go and have counselling without fear of it getting back to management", says Michelle Senecal de Fonseca.

In the IT and telecoms industry, "your job is always at risk – especially mid to upper management. There is a merger and all of a sudden the acquiring company comes in and some layers of management are booted out due to duplications and cost cuttings.

"There are constant reorganisations and new emerging technologies to learn and master, requiring you to keep pace. Therefore, the industry tends to keep people on the edge", she says.

You can end up suffering from an 'ambiguous loss', which is when you do not feel in control of your own destiny or you do not feel safe or you do not trust your leaders to answer you correctly.

How resilient you are as a manager may affect how well you cope when faced with the challenges of change, which we looked at in detail in Chapter 2. But you can learn how to adapt well and recover quickly after a stressful, traumatic or challenging event.

WHAT YOU CAN DO

- Build your own board of advisors. Having a network of influential supporters in work and externally will help you to keep perspective and also focus on your own career. A handful of strong connections is usually more beneficial than a large number of weaker acquaintances.

- Find a mentor and join a peer support group to widen your network.

- Learn techniques to manage negative thoughts and focus on the positives and even view life's challenges as opportunities.

- Take regular exercise to help reduce stress and anxiety.

- Finally, be kind to yourself and take a break. Switch off from the busyness of the day and focus your mind on something else such as a hobby, book, friends or meditation.

WHAT TO DO NEXT

1. Look at your soft skills toolkit, considering those mentioned: emotional intelligence, build trust with authenticity, credibility and empathy, influence and persuade, understand intrinsic needs, delegate and facilitate.

2. Choose three skills that you would like to work on. Write down what has to be improved and why, based on past and present experiences, with your digital transformation goals in mind. Reflect on how you can make this happen.

3. Put yourself forward for courses on the soft skills offered by your employer. Alternatively, make a business case for upskilling or take free online courses.

FURTHER READING

The Speed of Trust by Stephen Covey

The Power of Habit by Charles Duhigg

Dare to Lead by Brene Brown

The Manager's Path by Camille Fournier

Unleashed: The Unapologetic Leader's Guide to Empowering Everyone Around You by Frances X Frei and Anne Morriss

Management Teams: Why they Succeed or Fail by RM Belbin

Influence: The Psychology of Persuasion by Robert Cialdini

Beating burnout at work by Paula Davis

Scott Asia's TED Talk: Saving soft skills from extinction: www.mental-healthatwork.org.uk

FT series Mental Health at Work: Feeling the strain

CHAPTER 5

DATA MAGICIANS AND ROBO-BOSSES

D ata is everything today and digital transformation means using it and technology to drive change. "Data is the core of any business", says David Vivancos, a Spanish-based science and technology serial entrepreneur. "If there is no data, there is no business."

Here, we have focused on the people element of the data insights value chain and what the companies we spoke to did or are doing to introduce data analytics across the businesses and act on its insights. It is clear that no matter what line of work you are in, you will need to feel comfortable with how you use data and what it means for your role and team. Using data to drive your decisions can reveal important insights to make sure that you are fulfilling clients' needs based on behaviour or giving you the ability to make more accurate forecasts.

Examples can range from seeing what type of person is more likely to buy a product or service based on historical data, to banks evaluating lending risks to be selective about customer acquisition and who to market to and how.

Data is shaping the future of business across sectors, from personalised digital healthcare or online lessons to changing the way lawyers conduct business or whether a company opens a physical store in a particular town.

Digital information is being created, analysed and stored at an incredible rate, says the US Chamber of Commerce Foundation website: "90 per cent of the world's data has been produced in just the last two years. This explosion of information is known as 'Big Data', and it is completely transforming the world around us."

It is estimated that Google alone receives over 63,000 searches per second on any given day, according to the website seotribunal.com.

These are the technologies that are changing the world that we live in and this is how they are being used. Not only has the "sheer volume of available data grown exponentially" since 2013 and is expected to continue to do so, but also new tools have been developed for turning this "flood of raw data" into insights and action, according to a McKinsey report called "Achieving business impact with data".

The companies we spoke to are all grappling with data, whether it is forming a strategy, ensuring consistency or informing team leaders' decisions such as helping to drive news story decisions at the Financial Times, CNN, NZZ, DN and Nikkei to spotting trends in the legal sector at Hogan Lovells or understanding customer behaviour in financial services and banking, from Habito to Starling.

BUILD YOUR DATA FOUNDATIONS

Data can shape our business decisions before, during and after we take actions. As Carly Fiorina, the former chief executive of Hewlett-Packard, said: "The goal is to turn data into information, and information into insight".

"Data doesn't have to be this really complicated thing", says McKinley Hyden, who at the time of the interview was Head of Insights at the *Financial Times.*

Managed well, data is not noticed, but handled incorrectly and it could end up as reputational risk to the business and even hit revenue.

It is essential to get the right foundations in place, says Michelle Senecal de Fonseca, a senior executive at Citrix. If you do not have them you must start building them, she urges, "otherwise it will become too big a problem".

The way you begin to construct the foundation is by taking these three steps, according to professional services firm PwC:

1. **Understand the data** you have and that which you need to develop or acquire to create data-based insights.

2. **Organise that data.** Once you have understood it, you need to streamline and integrate it, which typically involves the cloud or other integration technologies.

3. **Build trust in the data.** It needs to be transparent and secure with good governance, with data quality and cleansing processes in place.

Global law firm Hogan Lovells had to work out its strategy as the business had "hundreds of thousands of clients" and so had a huge set of data, says Michael Davison, Deputy Chief Executive. "It is a challenge bringing that data into our space and to analyse it."

The type of questions they considered were:

■ Who owns the data in your firm?
■ Who maintains it?
■ How would you store it?
■ How would you structure it?
■ How do you build new data sets?
■ How do you use it?

The firm had people and customer intake systems, as well as confidential client information. "It's a challenge to join those pockets together", he says.

"It is a huge cultural shift that this data is now the firm's data and not an individual lawyer's data."

They had to get staff to buy into the concept that data is important and that collecting was not "just something that's optional". Working out the strategy was a "painful process" but it was "absolutely key", Davison says. "Data is now exploding left, right and center and people are becoming data owners in different ways every day" and as a result you need to stop things "spiraling out of control", he says.

SASWATI SAHA MITRA

Research Leader, Whatsapp, US-based messaging service

Insights from data are valuable but what do you do if you work at a company such as Whatsapp that has end-to-end encryption, meaning only the people talking to each other can see what is being shared? Despite privacy concerns at the messaging service owned by Facebook, researchers cannot collect user data.

Saswati Saha Mirta and her team have to rely on external insights which employees generate themselves. "We have a very different world where you have no data and you still have to be able to solve the problem relying a lot more on external insights", she says.

Take, for example, misinformation that was spread on Whatsapp during the pandemic or elections. They had to find a way to control the problem but they could not "just go in and pull this content out without disbanding what WhatsApp is". So they had to rely extensively on their internal community to crowdsource and asked questions such as what kind of misinformation are you seeing in your social groups?

"People are able to share that, and we are able to start extrapolating that", Mitra says.

But the company has no idea of what is in any message so employees have to go back to crowdsourcing that knowledge from WhatsApp or Facebook peers and ask them what they have seen in their communities. The research team also works with external users, where they ask them, for example, whether they have received information that looked suspect.

"It is self-reported data by users. But it gives us a reasonable signal that everything seems normal . . . or some information looks flaky", she says. "That gives

us a signal that something is definitely going on in this market, that our users are reporting back."

But Mitra does urge caution because there is "a high degree of self-reported data which is slightly less dependable than pure product analytics. But that's the best way we can ensure user privacy", she says.

HOW TO UNDERSTAND AND USE DATA

For the purposes of this section, we have assumed that the organisation you work for already has in place some form of data collection.

Using data to drive decision-making can help to improve an organisation's agility, aid quicker decisions to respond to business needs and spot opportunities for growth and recruitment needs. Managers can measure outcomes and also consider what action to take next. They can also understand their customers' needs and behaviours, identify what they are likely to buy next and develop or adjust products and services.

There are three key steps that managers should take when using data, according to Thomas H Davenport, co-author of *Keeping up with Quants,* and a professor of IT and management at Babson College in the US. He defined them as:

1. **Frame the question:** Define what you want to answer. If you frame the issue incorrectly, no amount of data will bring you to the right place. Recognise what the issue is and review previous findings as this will help you to frame it better. You need to be asking the right questions to be able to frame your business's problem, using data sets or breaking down the data to find the cause of any issues.

2. **Solve the problem:** Choose your variables, collect the data to measure them and then conduct analysis. You may not do the analysis yourself but your questions and insights will go a long way to help finding a solution.

3. **Present results to take action:** If you want anything to happen, you must communicate the results effectively. If a decision-maker does not understand the results or what they mean, they will not be comfortable making a decision based on them.

"It's your job to set up the question for your analysts and present their findings convincingly", he says in a *Harvard Business Review* video.

MANAGING BIAS

Many of the companies we spoke to have access to huge amounts of data, facts and information and some are at the point of trying to work out their data strategy. Not only that, they are trying to ensure their data is not biased or skewed, which if left unchecked can lead to problems of transparency and accountability.

"The usage of data is absolutely biased today", says Alberto Levy, international MBA professor and start-up mentor at IE Business School in Madrid. "You can direct the data interpretation to whatever bias you have."

One way to ensure a lack of bias on the research side is to think through your sampling.

When Saswati Saha Mitra was working on a Google research project in India, they took care to ensure the sampling came from a wide area, and not just the cities where internet connections were more stable. Ask yourself how well you are including a representative society in your sampling versus going for convenience and only contacting people in urban areas who can answer back to you using the internet, she says. It costs more money and time to ensure a much wider inclusion but the overall "holistic perspective" is really important. "But what is surprising . . . is sometimes I think we over-estimate differences, whereas the world is actually more similar."

On the product data side, where you could be looking at customer feedback, for example, "there could be bias for sure", she says. "We often see that a lot more men write in with their complaints than women. So there's definitely a skew there. I won't call it bias, because it's a choice that you are making to report or not report, but it is skewed because we are hearing more from men, we are hearing more from young people than older people."

You have to operate with what you are getting and solve the problem by working with the best possible data you have. But managing bias a little bit better when planning and doing research or analysis can go a long way to improving results. Companies no longer rely on so-called gut instinct even if the numbers can validate it to a large extent.

"There is no way back", says Nico Arcauz, Head of Smart Grids Global and Spain at Iberdrola. "There is no more gut feeling about a decision. It needs to be sustained by data or it will not be taken."

Starling uses machine learning and artificial intelligence in security and onboarding processes. "But it's so important that those models are audited because it is very easy for those models to become biased", says Anne Boden, Chief Executive.

Starling runs huge, "very complex" models, whereby the bank can determine certain outcomes by looking at the data, but those models have been trained on previous decisions, she says. "You have to be very, very careful . . . that you don't infer something."

MEETING CUSTOMERS' NEEDS

Others were trying to think of issues from the customer's perspective, from journalists to online jewellery retailers.

"Putting yourself in the customer's mind, the reader, the user is the only way to deliver what they want", says Robert Shrimsley, former Managing Editor of FT.com.

Sometimes you will need to go back to basics. "The innovation will probably naturally follow if you think about the end goal, what you're trying to achieve, and not get too stuck on the analytics", says Connie Nam, founder of online jewellery retailer Astrid & Miyu (see box on page 91).

The type of questions she considers to understand and meet customer needs are:

- What does your customer want?
- What are they looking for right now?
- What are you trying to sell?

The product development and merchandising team runs analysis daily. Items they consider include:

- What sold?
- What category?
- What colour?
- What collections?

"A lot of our product development is heavily driven by data on what the customer is looking for, what the customers have bought", says Nam. "This is mixed with customer feedback and trend forecasts of what is likely to happen in the market."

GAINING INSIGHTS AND VALUE

The McKinsey report mentioned earlier also noted that "data in its raw and most basic form is virtually worthless until we give it a voice by gleaning valuable insights from it. But how do we make data speak?"

The report identifies some key components that make up what it called the 'insights value chain':

- Data must be thought of as the whole process of collecting, linking, cleaning, enriching and augmenting information.

- Analytics describes the set of digital methodologies (such as software) deployed to extract insights, as well as employees capable of developing these methods.

- IT is the technical layer enabling the storing and processing of data.

- People from the front lines of sales to deep within the business are needed to run an analytics operation that turns data into insights and successfully implements them.

- Processes must be able to deliver at scale. Some might need to be adapted, others automated or made more agile.

Like Astrid & Miyu, Zoom Video Communications uses data to interpret where it should expand geographically. "We definitely look at data closely. We guide the business based on the trends we are seeing and, given the dramatic year in 2020, it caused us to think differently evaluating the potential in front of us, the speed in which we could go after it, and how to best capture the massive opportunity on hand", says Abe Smith, Head of International at Zoom.

How you use data day to day and in your business is key to maintaining a competitive edge whether you are in the education and health sectors or media and banking. News and media companies adept at using data in subscription and other consumer revenue models increased reader retention, conversion rates on paid products, and overall revenue per reader, a Deloitte report on data maturity noted.

"With the website you are getting constant feedback on the decisions you are taking and that is a constant process at a microlevel – a paragraph or picture", says Robert Shrimsley, the former Managing Editor of FT.com. "The information is there for you – what is working, giving you a much greater insight into your audience and what they want and what works for them. Since our business model has changed from an advertising model to a subscription model, what works for the audience is more important than it used to be and therefore putting yourself in the head of the reader is very important."

And in executive education and training, data is being used to work out what clients will want and what they think of the programmes. "We track data in all parts of the journey", says Gustaf Nordbäck, Chief Executive of

Headspring, a joint venture between the *Financial Times* and IE business school. It uses data to monitor:

- early prospecting
- marketing activities
- understanding the personas
- how clients interact with Headspring's content and participate in events
- understanding the design and delivery of the training journey
- learning impact.

Data "will only become more important", says Nordbäck. "It is crucial to help shape how we design and deliver the learning experiences with the greatest client impact."

As we can see, the use of data is becoming key for success and transformation of many companies. The broad strategies and processes may be similar but we have to personalise the information to our sector, company and project goals.

This also explains the explosion and fast growth of customer relationship management groups such as Salesforce which provides services that can manage and apply the data for you.

CONNIE NAM

Founder of Astrid & Miyu, online jewellery retailer

At Astrid & Miyu data very much drives business decisions, including which towns or countries the online retailer should plan to expand into physical stores.

For 2020, part of the company's strategy was to go international. "We have based the countries that we want to prioritise on where the website traffic and revenues are coming from. So those really big positions are also very much data driven", says Nam.

In the UK, she is also planning to open a couple of regional stores. "That decision has been driven by where our customers are coming from regionally in the UK, on our website", she says.

The business runs an application that shows a heat map of where people are going on the website. "We're constantly monitoring analytics behind our website

▶

to make things better", she says. So she knows that in the towns or countries they target she has customers waiting, as part of the business offering has a service component. "We do piercing, tattoos, bracelet weldings, which you can't buy online", she says.

While other physical retailers are struggling in a tough economic outlook, Nam is "hopeful and optimistic". "I think a lot of businesses need to understand what the triggers are in getting people into the doors of physical retail. "You can't just be selling products. I think you need to offer something else other than the products because it's so easy to shop online now. And a lot of people are not used to shopping online."

EXERCISE

You should consider how to leverage data to optimise business results and make decisions based on data that is reliable and meaningful for your company. More organisations are building their own data teams instead of relying on third-party partners and sources.

Following on from the insights value chain, write down the answers to these questions to reflect on and start using data:

1. How can you start to collect data? What data is relevant and appropriate for your project and how can you obtain it? Think of the simplest and most cost-effective methods. If you have no or little budget, use open data – that can be used and reused – to capture the overall, global picture.

2. What software or digital tools do you already have in place that can provide you with data sets?

3. Where can you store this data safely?

4. What are the legal issues to deal with?

5. Who are the best professionals in your team to collate, safeguard and make sense of this data to be able to use it practically?

6. What actions can you take based on the data collected?

7. How can you prepare to scale the use of data?

HOW DATA DRIVES CULTURE CHANGE

Data is also driving a cultural shift in how traditional roles are carried out. Lawyers who were once reactive, waiting for clients to contact them, are now having to be proactive, informing clients of trends. And managers of sales forces are no longer leaders of 'sellers' but leaders of 'selling'.

"Traditionally people came to us for legal advice. Now we use data to predict things. Clients want to know the trends. What do we see in the market place and what's coming up?" says Michael Davison of Hogan Lovells.

"We now go to clients and say: 'We've seen this data, you're in this field, this is likely to happen to you'", and then the firm can advise them on how to position themselves for Brexit, Covid or any other risk, he says. "We really make sure we are processing data to make our service better."

Separately, the law firm is also partnering with university students in data science to use them as a testbed to develop those skills. It also gives the firm a chance to see people it may want to recruit.

Similarly at Citrix, roles are going to change. "I keep telling my team at the moment we are leaders of sellers but we are going to become leaders of selling and selling is going to be a process that is data-driven to find your pipeline to engage and move on", says Michelle Senecal de Fonseca, a senior executive.

At Citrix they had developed a predictive tool to see who the people were in a buying cycle. This tool tells them:

- Were they looking at the products or at you or your competitors?
- Were they looking into the websites about a particular topic?

Citrix had a scoring system to see where its sales people should spend more time to reach potential customers. "So pleased we had spent the time doing that over the past two years [2018–20] because if you think about the primary driver of good sales people, it's that they like to be physically interacting with their customers", says Senecal de Fonseca.

"During a pandemic when no one's allowed to be anywhere except in front of a computer, how do you find your customers? How do you engage with them? These predictive tools start to show you where people have activity."

Some companies were trying to work out who the data owners were and carried out data audits so they could build links between them.

The ownership of data is something that Tom Fortin, Chief Operating Officer at iCapital Network, a US-based financial technology platform, knows only too well. From his previous experience of digital transformation across the financial services sector, he says "controlling and hiding data is the number one way of creating politics inside an organisation".

"When you create transparency and data, you really find the people who are highly political in the organisation that want to control and hide their own data. Those are the people who object [because] . . . they're losing control of their data. But the organisation benefits massively."

MCKINLEY HYDEN

Head of Insights, *Financial Times* (2019–20)

When McKinley Hyden was sent into the FT newsroom to establish data analytics, she took the approach that she was supposed to "get the dinosaurs in editorial to see the light". But after several months of making little progress she realised that "was just not a helpful attitude to have".

So she had to reassess how she was going about introducing change and started to listen and understand editorial's perspectives. "What I really needed to do was spend time talking and listening about how decisions were being made and what the incentives were. Because you can't change behaviour unless you know what the incentives are. That was really pivotal", she says.

The way she got herself known and data as a topic of conversation was to speak to different news desks. "Editorial was more questioning than other departments", she says. "I got asked some really pointed questions around an index I was using and I was so unaccustomed to being asked those kinds of questions [that I had] to take a step back and think: why did I use that index?"

One of the conversations Hyden had with a head of a news desk led to "a significant piece of data that is used in the newsroom" – the quality reads metric, which included time spent on page, the number of page views and scroll depth.

Hyden had asked the news editor what type of information would be useful to her. "She was saying we have page views but we have some content that we know will never get a ton of page views but we know it's important. How can you help show which things are like that? That was an astute thing to say", says Hyden.

Having those conversations was important but so was holding presentations to show her data 'wares'. "If you just say: tell me what good looks like, you can't do that. People don't know what to say. If they don't know what the data even looks like, it's really hard to have that conversation.

"You have to do both: you have to say here's what the data looks like and you have to find a way to show it. This is what we can tell you about your desk, this is how the data can help you. How can the data be more helpful to you and what's the news you can use here? And what's missing?"

WHAT CAN GO WRONG

Data is only as good as the insights you gain from it and you do need to be cautious as there is such a thing as bad data.

For example, in one of the biggest miscarriages of justice in British legal history, hundreds of former post office workers were convicted of theft, fraud and false accounting after the Horizon IT system installed by the Post Office and supplied by Fujitsu, a Japanese computer company, falsely suggested there were cash shortfalls, the *Guardian* reported.

Dozens of workers were subsequently cleared by the court of appeal in 2021, clearing the way for many of the other 700 sub-postmasters to challenge their convictions too.

In his written judgement, Lord Justice Holyroyde said: "Defendants were prosecuted, convicted and sentenced on the basis that the Horizon data must be correct, when in fact there could be no confidence as to that foundation."

While the above example of when things go wrong could be seen as an outlier, the world of data is "insane", says Alberto Levy, of IE business school in Spain, because you can do "whatever you want" with it. "We have these huge data sets, then we just massage them to do whatever you want, and justify our actions based on the data", he says.

Many of the companies we spoke to were looking at the consistency of their data, that is the measurement of variables throughout the datasets, and its collection across different departments and countries, from the legal sector to software and financial services.

When Tom Fortin was Managing Director at BlackRock, to achieve consistent data they needed "to focus the enterprise system on one database with one process on one system. That's the key, you have to have those three things together. You've got to have consistency and process. And you can only have that by having one database.

"And then you have to have everyone focused on one system, and you create that co-dependency, and you create transparency of the data and the process at any one time."

Meanwhile, law firm Hogan Lovells found its biggest data set was in the US and UK – and it was pretty homogenous across those countries. But as soon as you widened the net, it was "harder to get that consistency", says Michael Davison, Deputy Chief Executive.

One reason for this is that the legal requirements and restrictions on data privacy vary worldwide. One of the most important pieces of legislation is the General Data Protection Regulation in the European Union. It covers the collection, use, transmission and security of data in 27 member states of the European Union. For the complete guide on GDPR, go to the following website: https://gdpr.eu.

The UK has retained the GDPR in domestic law but can keep the framework under review.

According to the information Commissioner's Office, the type of restriction GDPR covers in the UK includes:

- Individuals have the right to request the restriction or suppression of their personal data.

- When processing is restricted, you are permitted to store the personal data but not use it.

- An individual can make the request verbally or in writing.

- You have one calendar month to respond to a request.

Meanwhile, the US does not have one federal law governing data but there are laws for example on health and credit information.

The Federal Trade Commission, a US government agency, also ensures consumer data protection. Its website warns businesses to be clear about what they do with consumer data. For more information on what the FTC covers, go to www.ftc.gov/tips-advice.

China is also looking at introducing personal data protection, and draft proposals have some similarities to the GDPR.

And in Africa, as of 2019, out of 54 countries, 25 had passed data protection laws, while others had introduced bills that were under consideration, according to a Hogan Lovells article on the website lexology.com.

What this all means for firms like Hogan Lovells is that on issues, say, relating to diversity and inclusion, "we can gather as much data as we like on that in the UK and in the US" but in the EU it is difficult to hold regarding individual ethnicity due to GDPR.

And it did take the firm three goes at getting the strategy right, which was a challenge in itself. "We need to be super careful around the quality of the data", Davison says. "For client profiling for 2021, we used algorithms. But you need to cross-check against the algorithms, otherwise you can get dodgy results."

To illustrate the point he gives a generic example of an organisation that had a recruitment database and over ten years the company hired 1,000 people. Out of that group, employees from College A had been successful hires but those from College B had not.

"That is a real problem because you will recruit the same people, who act the same, look the same and that is concreting in recruitment decisions that are no longer appropriate", he says. "Even blind recruitment needs checks and balances. The data will only take you so far. You need humans to challenge it."

And even with machine learning, where an algorithm improves through use of data, which Hogan Lovells uses to plough possibly thousands of documents through to produce a map of a case, "you will always need a human in the background, checking", says Davison.

Senecal de Fonseca agrees that you still need humans to cross-check the data as you can encounter problems with how data has been inputted. "We've had to build business intelligence tools with predictive analytics over the last three or four years. However, even then you can't solely rely on the data outputs as some of the input data came from historic corporate sources which may have been inaccurate or incomplete or there are biases that need to be watched for in the AI algorithms so you don't get unintended consequences", she says.

"You still have to have somebody who understands the business, can question what the data is saying and interpret the business outcomes. We are getting better at it and I believe a lot of companies are going through the same learning curve."

Meanwhile in the health sector, machine learning has also had a "huge impact", says Kanwarjit Singh, healthcare executive and oncology physician in the US, where it is used to look at data sets and pick up variables.

But errors can and do occur. It was also not all plain sailing for McKinley Hyden, Head of Insights at the FT, when she was working on a newsroom data project for a new content section on the website, and realised there was an "actioned error in the logic which was reversing the numbers". The desk had been making many decisions based on those numbers and thought they were doing well. But she had to tell them that "the opposite of what they thought was true. And that was not great", she says.

NICO ARCAUZ

Head of Smart Grids Global and Spain, Iberdrola, Spanish utility

A "goldmine of data" has helped the Spanish utility not only to anticipate problems such as power outages in the network but also to reduce fraud.

"There are still a few customers who still steal from us", says Arcauz. "And there are also non-customers who connect to the network illegally and that also increases the losses."

Before the digital transformation of smart meters, households were randomly selected for spot checks. Now these types of campaigns are more successful and are much more focused. Now Iberdrola can use the data from the meters to make a balance and subtract the total consumption of the customers in a particular neighbourhood and subtract that amount to the one meter that is up the line.

By analysing data on an area of the network where losses "are much higher than what they should be", the company can direct its resources in the field to the houses to control any potential fraud.

Iberdrola is only just starting to generate value from data. From a business perspective the losses control and fraud detection tool is one of the ways it is benefiting from the project Acauz oversaw. "We are sitting on a goldmine of data", he says, and they are using analytics so that they cannot only correct when the asset goes down but they "have preventive solutions to try to take action prior to that asset malfunctioning".

All the data that the company is collecting from the meters is also good for modelling the network and prioritising investments as well as giving reporting incidents automatically.

Customers are also provided with valuable data so that they can manage their consumption online and they have better information to make decisions around energy efficiency.

And the quality of supply is a big bonus as the service can be restored much faster than in the past. The company has seen a 25 per cent improvement with customers now going without power for 45 minutes a year. Not only that, the company has used data to anticipate the reaction to outages and the number of claims has gone down dramatically.

"The message is that we have deployed technology . . . with a focus on making our business more efficient but at the same time focusing on the customer, providing the services to the customer and helping them to have informed decisions about the power they contract", he says.

WHAT TO DO NEXT

1. Find out what your organisation's data strategy is and how it aligns with business priorities.

2. Identify ways to relate your work to it and come up with some quick wins to improve it. One way you could look to add value, for example, is by analysing customer churn and think about how to reduce this turnover.

3. With help from internal and external stakeholders, frame a question about what further data is needed and where it will come from to reach goals so that any follow-up actions are useful and effective.

FURTHER READING

Data: A Guide to Humans by Phil Harvey and Noelia Jimenez Martinez

Data Analytics made Accessible by Anil Maheshwari

Too Big to Ignore: The Business Case for Big Data by Paul Simon

Keeping up with the Quants by Thomas H Davenport and Jin-Ho Kim

Automate or be automated by David Vivancos

CHAPTER 6

THE REAL POWER OF DIVERSITY

Having a diverse and inclusive workforce is key for businesses to succeed at digital transformation. This is because employees will help to not only increase market share worldwide but also create products that work for everyone.

Here we give you proactive steps that go beyond recruitment, giving you advice on how to build commitment and engagement with diverse members of your team as well as how to really include them, ensuring their voices are heard and enabling them to progress at work.

Diversity initiatives are still relatively new in businesses today and they can often sit on the fringes of strategies and plans. Yet it is vital that companies get to grips with them because their customers, staff and potential talent hires are looking for them. But it can often fall to managers to make diversity policies work because they are the ones who have to activate the strategy and they will be responsible for them day to day.

And be warned, this is often where issues can start. It is at this level in an organisation where these policies can fail to gain traction, especially when flat internal departmental structures make it difficult to progress, or pressure on headcount means extra resources are hard to come by.

"That is where we see a lot of the issues around diversity and inclusion at that level. And it also links back to resource", says Priscilla Baffour, who at the time of the interview was Global Head of Diversity and Inclusion at the Financial Times.

Tom Ogletree, Vice-President of Social Impact at General Assembly, a leading education company based in the US, agrees: "When companies have made all sorts of bold claims and commitments to diversity, equity and inclusion from the C-suite, this doesn't always flow through an organisation down to the recruiter level, or the hiring manager level, who are incentivised to be risk-averse."

Diverse teams reflect the company's market and give insights into customers' personas so that their needs are met more effectively. This in turn hones the design of innovative products and services. Not only that, it can also affect the bottom line – positively. For example, a 2018 report by McKinsey, a professional services company, found that companies in the top 25th percentile for gender diversity were 21 per cent more likely to experience higher than average profits.

The challenge for managers around diversity is that they are going to have to manage people who are very different. This means they are going to have to work harder to meet their team's needs in order to support them so that they can perform at their best.

WHAT IS DIVERSITY AND INCLUSION?

Diversity and inclusion are closely related but they are two separate areas. The former not only encompasses gender, race, socio-economic background, education and religion but also communication and working styles as well as personality types, different levels of experience and ages in teams and disabilities – all of which affect how people work together.

It can also include more subtle dimensions such as where you physically work altering your perspective.

"It's about people from all walks of life and experiences existing in one place together and that difference is respected and valued", says Baffour. "As a leader and a manager, it is being able to tap into that diversity of thought and diversity of experience and ask whose voice is missing."

Inclusivity, on the other hand, is creating a collaborative atmosphere at work where everyone feels empowered to speak up at meetings and have their ideas heard. It is the process whereby organisations truly integrate employees, teams and departments and allow for differences to be explored in a positive and nurturing way.

"For me, it is not just about those characteristics of race and disability, but also different personality styles and different ways of thinking", she says. "For businesses to be truly innovative, you need people who have different styles and ways of working. We can't all be extroverts who love networking." In order for us to see the real value of diversity and inclusion we need to create spaces for employees to be their authentic selves, she says.

Inclusive leaders who do this well tend to develop the skill of cultural competency in the same way they may have known their project management or their budgeting. They get to know people who are different from themselves and they make an effort to do so.

"Not enough businesses are highlighting that their leaders need to be good at that", says Femi Otitoju, who founded the UK-based Challenge Consultancy in 1985.

It's important to put shared values first, rather than age, gender or experience. Otherwise, you risk building homogenous teams with a similar outlook.

WHY ARE THEY IMPORTANT FOR INNOVATION?

The Black Lives Matter protests that expanded globally after the murder of George Floyd by a US police officer in 2020 galvanised many corporations to tackle the lack of diversity in their organisations. Companies recognised that to serve all their customer groups worldwide, they had to be able to understand them and not have bias against them in their workforces.

"It was this inflection point", says Liz Lowe, Head of Community Engagement at Adobe. As the conversation around diversity and inclusion (D&I) in the tech industry in particular intensified, the social impact team at the US-based software company saw an opportunity to align scholarships and apprenticeships with increasing demand for more diverse talent.

One of the reasons more diverse teams can move the dial on profit is that they can build on their collective life experiences to collaborate. This creates a powerful group of employees that enables a company not only to succeed but reap the benefits of people who feel like they belong.

"They bring their life experience and are more likely to think differently to those that have come through the same old routes and think 'same old, same old'", says Otitoju. Lowe agrees. There is "more innovation around products when you have different points of view involved", she says.

Customer satisfaction can also increase because serving the end-user of a product can be hard if the decision-makers in a company do not include people who can relate to the client.

In the news business, for example, media companies are seeing a huge amount of disruption and fragmentation in terms of how people consume news.

"We have much more competition in the market. All these changes impact our business commercially, how we distribute our content to readers and how the content is paid for and how we build in a more diverse readership so that is how the strategy connects for us", says Baffour. "In order for us to diversify our content, we need our workforce to be diverse as well."

MERI WILLIAMS

Former Chief Technology Officer at Monzo, a challenger bank (2018–20) and Head of Delivery at UK Government Digital Service (GDS) (2012–13)

Meri Williams has a lot of first-hard experience of where diverse workforces enhance products and improve customers' lives. "I'm a woman working in tech, I'm queer and godless and I'm neuro diverse and I have a disability", she says.

At GDS she worked with a blind coder on a project about assistance for people who lack digital access or skills where "we started to care about mobile phone usage and also people with different accessibility requirements." They also looked at things such as where you could use a mobile phone one-handed because you may have a child "on your hip or your shoulder is dislocated".

"It was embarrassing when a team was too homogenous and so they hadn't thought of really basic things", she says. But "there were fewer issues if the team was diverse – if your hands shake a bit, touch screen is not going to work."

At Monzo, a vulnerable customers' team decided to work on a project to help gambling addicts. "We could block transactions that looked like gambling transactions and it could help survivors of addiction", she says. "There were people in that team who were gambling survivors and a lot of really good work came out of there – the gambling block."

"If you wanted to get [the block] switched off, you had to get in touch with customer services – and they make you wait 24 hours. They aren't going to say no but they are going to give you a cooling-off period. Then the next day, after 24 hours, they ask whether you are sure you want it switched off. It does result in a lower relapse rate."

LESS ROOM FOR MISTAKES

Diverse businesses are also "less likely to make mistakes that are going to upset the community because you have checks and balances inside", Otitoju says. "So you have an edge because you have people who think differently."

In terms of innovation, companies can risk reputational damage if their new products do not work for everyone in the global marketplace. This can range from healthcare to automobile and technology sectors, to name a few. The website Digital Trends, for example, reported there have been questions over the accuracy of optical heart rate monitors on wearables when taking readings on different skin tones. NBC News also reported that Apple became embroiled in 'Tattoogate' when its watch did not work as well on people with dark tattoos.

Similarly, while driverless cars may know the difference between left and right, they may not be able to spot 'non-white" and 'non-male faces, the *Sunday Times* reported.

The UK's Law Commission in a consultation paper on automated vehicles found that bias had "sometimes crept into the design of vehicles and automated systems". "Air bags save many lives, but the first generation of air bags posed risks to smaller passengers because they were developed with adult males in mind. Current facial recognition software may apply more accurately to white, male faces", it noted.

Meanwhile, Google launched an equitable camera initiative to change its computational photo algorithms to address long-standing problems, according to a report on the *Guardian* website.

Kodak's Shirley Cards had been used by photo labs for calibrating skin tones, shadows and light in photographs. The card, named after the original model who worked for Kodak, ensured Shirley looked good, to the detriment of people with darker skin colour, it reported.

EXERCISE

This exercise will help you discover how your team matches your client's diversity and turn your understanding and empathy into tangible results.

Look at your innovation team and see how it reflects the group you are trying to serve.

A model developed by Lee Gardenswartz and Anita Rowe is a clear way to see how four layers of diversity play their part.

These layers are:

Organisational – the type of work, hierarchy and status, such as management

External – geographical location, income, education, habits, religion, marital status and appearance

Internal – age, race, gender, race, physical abilities and ethnic origin

Personality – this is at the core.

Reflect on who your target market is and what their diversity make-up looks like using the four layers of the model.

If you see much mismatch with your team, it could be useful to suggest conducting more focus groups or interviews with stakeholders to draw together a broader perspective and input into a project before any further investment of time, money and resources.

The more information you have upfront, the better your solution will be and you will be able to reduce the risk of failure or the need to make big adjustments later.

WHAT YOU CAN DO AT THE HIRING STAGE

You can take several steps to create an environment where diverse employees have a voice so they are helping to shape the organisation's structures, its interactions, its talent and not necessarily joining a company at the bottom rung.

First, starting at recruitment, you should ensure that you are going beyond that equal opportunities statement at the end of the advert, by doing the following:

- Re-examine the criteria for roles and question whether they are essential skills. "If you're looking for the same things using the same words, you're going to get the same people", says Otitoju. "Stop saying you must have a degree from X university. It is also about what traits we're looking for." Tom Ogletree at GA agrees: "One thing that we have seen time and time again is that students who do not fit a particular mould or do not check a certain set of boxes, find themselves screened out early."

- Promote your job adverts on social media sites used by different communities.

- Be clear on job adverts that you are looking for people under-represented in your organisation.

- Offer flexibility, whether that is where you work, or when, "to make sure parents can care for their children and do their job", says Elyssa Byck, co-founder and Chief Operating Officer at Kindred, a US-based executive membership network focused on the future of socially responsible business.

- Hire people from under-represented communities into decision-making roles.

"You don't have to discriminate in favour of a particular group of people. You have to work out what it is that those people might bring you and work out how much you value it", says Otitoju.

You may have to reassess entry-level roles and create one that did not exist before. Adobe, for example, created positions in areas such as web development and data science, and set aside resources for someone to transition into these fields.

If, however, you do not have the budget to hire employees into your team, you can still do the following:

- Reach out to employee resource groups and make a few key connections.

- Build yourself a support group so that when a job vacancy does come up you are more prepared to change the job profile to attract a wider range of people to apply.

LIZ LOWE

Head of Community Engagement, Adobe, US-based software company

Adobe took an agile approach, applying a mindset of fail fast, iterate and review to develop a programme to increase diversity in the software company.

This gave hiring managers a framework that they understood within their field. "I tried to approach it from a design thinking model where I was interviewing hiring managers and making them a part of the building process", says Liz Lowe.

Some of them had told her they did not have a wide enough talent pool to hire engineers from diverse backgrounds at the highest level. So she worked with them to build an apprenticeship programme, the Adobe Digital Academy, to develop the technical talent in web development, data science and user experience design that could be hired by the company.

She admits those initial conversations were "really hard" as it required a mindset shift in hiring practices. It took a combination of the HR team leading the charge and some managers stepping up to make change happen.

One leader in particular, who had his own experience of growing up in an under-resourced community, was crucial to proving it could work. "He hired a woman full time from the programme, who is still with Adobe and on our Photoshop team as an engineer. His reputation and his success with this one case allowed other hiring managers to say: 'I can try this', says Lowe.

She has seen managers make the most effective mindset shift just by stepping up and realising it can be "new and uncomfortable to work with someone from a non-traditional background, but that is diversity, and that is being inclusive. You can take it step by step . . . but at some point, you just need to actually hire someone that comes from a different background than you do. You need to recognise that many skills are coachable."

Since Adobe started the programme in 2016, the company has hired about 60 per cent of candidates as full-time employees and half of them were promoted within their first year. Other students went on to high-paying roles at tech companies elsewhere in the US.

"So they are going on to be leaders on their teams and make hiring decisions to influence the product and the future of the company", she says.

COLLECT THE DATA AND DRIVE STRATEGY

To be successful at delivering on diversity policies, data collection within a company is critical. Without the data collection, companies will not understand where the issues are and where to focus their efforts. Many D&I initiatives can fail because they are seen as tick-box exercises and they are not aligned to business strategy. "They are almost copied and pasted initiatives from other organisations", says Baffour.

But to succeed, companies should come up with their own tailor-made individual ways of assessing diversity.

One of the challenges – and biggest achievements – Baffour faced was collecting employee demographic data. It was important because by doing that, she could develop a strategy to improve the diversity of the workforce and measure progress.

In 2018, at the FT only 26 per cent of people had disclosed their ethnicity data. By September 2020, that had increased to 83 per cent. This meant the company could not only publish the ethnicity pay gap but that it could "start to really understand where some of the issues" were by breaking down that data. The laws on collecting data do differ worldwide. You can read more on data regulation in Chapter 5.

Be prepared that people may resist this change. It can be partly fear of the unknown as they ask if the data is going to be used against them.

"A lot of what I did was educating, encouraging people, and building that trust", says Baffour. She had to reassure people along the following lines:

- Who can see the data?
- Who is responsible?
- What is it going to be used for?

In your company, you could:

- Look at where data is being collected from. Is there an issue with people filling in the form?
- Work with senior leadership and managers on internal communication and internal PR to help collect the data.
- Set a goal or target for data collection.

"Ultimately, if we were to be a better, more inclusive organisation, then this data would help us to get there and it was consistently delivering that message", she says.

She created a guide that explained why they were asking each question and what they would use that information for. The data can help you to build a picture of what is happening across an organisation and enable you to identify patterns that you may be able to change, such as people from certain ethnic minorities leaving the company.

PRISCILLA BAFFOUR

Global Head of Diversity and Inclusion, Financial Times Group (2019–21)

When Priscilla Baffour joined the Financial Times *she had a mission to move the dial on diversity and inclusivity across the media company. At first she spent time not only looking at the data but also capturing the "lived experience", listening to people about what it was like to work in the organisation. She built relationships, finding out what people were passionate about and linking her strategy to this.*

Then she connected diversity and inclusion to the overall business strategy. "Ensure it is not just a standalone, somewhere over there in HR and that it is connected to the wider business. That is key", she says.

The steps she took included:

- **Reverse mentoring:** *"A really useful tool in driving cultural change".* The Next Generation Board was set up to help drive this initiative and connect with the FT's board members. It was made up of a diverse team from across the company who aimed to give a different perspective on strategy. It was *"great way to break down those invisible barriers between leadership and other members of staff".*

- **Growth of employee resource groups:** She worked with these groups on their strategy and their business plans and that fed into the wider D&I strategy.

- **Mandatory training on inclusive leadership:** These sessions were made mandatory because *"at times it can feel like preaching to the choir".* Those that are passionate about change always attended. *"Those that aren't, won't",* she says. Inclusion and diversity is about everyone. *"Every manager, everyone in the organisation has a responsibility to be aware of how their behaviour can impact other people and how they feel. All it takes is one person to say or do the wrong thing and it affects the culture of the company",* she says.

  "We all have so many habits where we are used to doing things in a certain way. It is uncomfortable at times to ask people to do things in a different way. So unlearn those old habits and relearn again."

- **Growth at all levels:** The aim was to diversify the talent pool and start engagement with talent at entry level through apprenticeships and internships as well as tackle under representation at every layer of the organisation. Jobs were advertised in diverse spaces and managers were requested to have 'mixed' shortlists of candidates for the interview stage. *"So as not to take a generation to achieve diversity, the answer is in recruitment",* she says.

"Historically, people have said the talent is not there. And that's why it's important to collect the data, we could see that at times there was a pipeline issue but managers' biases were creeping in. So having that data is crucial to really understand where the issues are."

"We all have that [unconscious] bias but it creeps in when you can't track as well. In the creative industries it is all very subjective: 'They are not quite there yet'; 'They are not the right fit'. Sometimes when you write that stuff down, you start to realise it's your biases creeping in."

HOW TO BUILD INCLUSIVE TEAMS

Once you have hired an inclusive team, you will need to be proactive about creating an inclusive environment to ensure that all voices are heard. The steps you can take include:

- Being clear on commitment to them. Let them know where you stand and how supportive you might be about particular issues that are important to them.

- Being brave with your engagement with them, telling them you want to hear their views. Give them a clear signal that you mean well, with good intent, and they are likely to tell you more easily what they need. "Just say, I want to hear what you have to say. Because you're different from me. And I need it. Just be upfront about it", says UK-based consultant Femi Otitoju.

- Facilitating their participation at team meetings, encouraging them to speak out.

- Showing your own vulnerabilities. "I am seeing people who have been managing for 40 years being much more willing to be open and vulnerable leaders. Just to show that you have flaws and vulnerabilities, doesn't mean that people won't follow you", says Otitoju.

One way to do this is to invite your team to take part in 'uninterrupted speaking time' (UST). This is a mediation tool that can be used to establish psychological safety so that every 'different one' has equal say. You can start using it by doing the following:

- Ask each team member to start any conversation.
- Give them a few minutes to share their thoughts.
- Then start a discussion.

This sets a framework for everyone to contribute, including anyone with a more introverted personality. In this way, healthy dialogue is created from the outset.

"You need to have a psychologically safe environment for people. It is OK to have a different opinion. It is OK to challenge", says Gustaf Nordbäck, Chief Executive of Headspring, a joint venture between the *Financial Times* and IE Business School.

"You need to nurture diversity of thought within the organisation", he says. "This is a crucial ingredient of an organisation that embodies a growth mindset, and where you can stimulate creativity and innovation."

Nneile Nkholise, founder of 3D-IMO, a South African start-up that automates livestock data analytics, agrees: "The reason why diversity is important for businesses is that it creates a more inclusive culture where everyone is appreciated based on their unique qualities."

If this environment is not created, some team members may feel unheard and stop contributing. Over time, this can lead to misunderstanding and conflict.

"It's no good having a token woman or black person there and all they are doing is cowering in the corner. They've got to be able to feel they can contribute and that they can challenge", says Otitoju.

"Managers are often a bit wary . . . you finally get a woman returner, or someone who identifies as something that you haven't had before. And then you don't talk about it. You say to your colleagues: 'I don't want to make them stand out.' Well, they know what they are", she says.

EXERCISE

In your next team meeting, use the uninterrupted speaking time method by asking all of your colleagues to speak for two to three minutes about their initial thoughts about a project you are working on.

Emphasise that this time is reserved for each member to express their views to ensure everyone's voice is heard.

Only after they have done that, enter into a debate.

Further steps you can take to be proactive about creating and building a D&I culture include:

- Talk to your team about what they are doing about it and make it the responsibility of staff to contribute.
- Make an effort to talk to minority staff, particularly those that have solo status in a team – and not just in your department.
- Review where your team or organisation is at and make recommendations for change.
- Have conversations across the company to hear other people's ideas about what needs to change.
- Become a mentor to support colleagues internally or offer your expertise externally. If you do not have time, find advocates across the business who can help you to champion fresh collaborations.

"In these very polite environments we don't talk about difference enough and we don't listen to those people because we don't encourage them to speak about it", says Otitoju. "We've got to acknowledge where we are, speak to those people and be guided by the sorts of things they might mention."

Baffour agrees. She held conversations across the FT organisation and what she picked up was that at every level from entry to the top, "there was this strong appetite from the business to broaden our diversity goals and targets" and to look at race and ethnicity in particular.

THE ROLE OF UNCONSCIOUS BIAS

It is important to realise that everyone has biases. We are shaped and conditioned by our experiences of what we feel is basically safe or unsafe as our brains are hardwired for survival.

But our initial reaction to people can change over time. When we have more access to diversity, it helps us to have a broader perspective towards our teams and also external stakeholders.

Unconscious bias is a preference or prejudice that is in favour of or against a particular person or group. It can occur automatically when someone makes quick judgements based on past experience. This compares with conscious bias which is deliberate prejudice.

These views of bias may not be right or reasonable. According to Acas, the UK's advisory, conciliation and arbitration service, they include when a person thinks:

- better of someone because they are alike
- less of someone because they are different in terms of race, religion or age.

This means they could make a decision influenced by false beliefs or assumptions. On Acas's website this can be called 'stereotyping'.

Take the venture capital industry. An article published in *Harvard Business Review* reported that it is "staggeringly homogeneous".

Start-up founders Nneile Nkholise and Anastasia Leng experienced the detrimental effect of homogeneity. They separately encountered sexism when they were trying to raise funds for their businesses, resulting in a much harder path for them to finance their projects.

Nkholise says she decided to stop raising investment funds in her first business after she was sent a sexist email, and combined with the attitude of male investors that made her feel "uncomfortable".

Meanwhile, Leng believes she was turned down for funds because she was pregnant, despite presenting a plan where she intended to take only six weeks' maternity leave, two of which were over the festive holidays and for the remainder, she was going to be available for emails, phone calls and so on. The justification the investors gave her, delivered by a female partner, was "they were unsure I would want to go back to work after having had a child", she says. "It's upsetting but this fundamentally means they are not the right partner and so we need to find someone who will not see gender and sex as a limiting factor to company growth."

"People are more likely to invest with people who look like them because you remind them of other people who are successful. This is why sometimes it tends to be a problem for women or [ethnic] minority founders to get the funding that white male alphas get.

"So there are fewer of us and that pattern of recognition just isn't as well formed. I think the best way to combat that is to elevate stories of successful female and minority founders who are making a business work and are returning investors capital with significant multipliers because that is the only thing that will change perception."

Nkholise agrees and believes the situation is beginning to change as more women become investors themselves and the tech ecosystem is starting to open up generally.

"We are seeing male investors being empathic to the challenges that women are facing", she says.

HOW TO IMPROVE YOUR AWARENESS

When it comes to unconscious bias, you will need to recognise that for any training to be of real benefit, it has to be ongoing and long term to stand a chance at leading to a lasting shift in behaviour.

This is a contentious area because there is a lack of evidence on how effective the training is. For example, the UK government announced at the end of 2020 that it was discontinuing its unconscious bias programme in various departments.

Having said that, one way of tackling bias, according to Elyssa Byck, a former BuzzFeed executive, is to build an environment of respect and dignity and this "starts with the individual". Byck suggests the following:

- Challenge existing assumptions and question whether something makes you feel uncomfortable. "Really approach these issues head on."

- Recognise privilege. Understand "that that might be the core of a lot of our challenges".

- Have conversations about race "which are hard conversations to have". You may need to bring in a facilitator into a session such as this.

"We want to, as companies, avoid performative ally-ship, making sure that we're not just making statements and that we are actually taking actions", she says.

Kindred, the executive membership network company, ensures team members all enter the conversation on 'one playing field', and they have an expert in the room to guide that conversation where everyone can speak on an equal level.

"Starting from a place of self-recognition is critical for leaders, because it allows everyone else to come up with their vulnerabilities and start from a place of learning", Byck says.

EXERCISE

You can take the Harvard implicit association test to discover your unconscious biases. The test says it can help you to penetrate two types of hiding identified by psychologists, whether that is something from others or unconsciously something from yourself.

The test has been criticised on the grounds that your bias can change according to when you take it. Having said that, you can find the tests at https://implicit. harvard.edu/implicit/takeatest.html.

Afterwards, write down your reflections on what these tests reveal about yourself and how you can become more aware of your biases.

STEER THE WAY UP THE CAREER LADDER

It is important to connect D&I to company values, says Priscilla Baffour, because employees are looking for different things when they join an organisation. "They want to come to a space where they know they can progress, where they know their ideas will be valued and respected. The world has changed and moved on", she says.

Be aware, though, that these initiatives can take time for people to progress up the career ladder and can even hinder the progression of others.

A study published in the *Strategic Management Journal* found that once a few women had been promoted quickly into top jobs, by skipping steps in the job ladders, faster advancement generally slowed and that "support for advancement was indeed a company choice, unfortunately one driven by public appearances".

Employers interested in increasing the diversity of their executive ranks should pay attention not only to who is in those jobs but also how long it took them to get there, the study said.

Longevity of service can hinder progression. If people stay at a company for decades, it is challenging to bring in new talent. Having said that, you can take these steps to help a colleague progress:

1. Check that is what they want and build trust. "There's something about showing that you understand, that allows people to trust you. If they trust you, you know about what's going on for them before it gets too big to deal with", says Otitoju.

2. Work with your HR department to make sure you understand whether there are any patterns as to why people leave or why they are not progressing as quickly as desired. "I see that in a lot of places, for example, black and minority ethnic people, particularly black people of Caribbean and Caribbean descent, tend to stay less long, leave sooner, and have fewer progression opportunities than their white counterparts", says Otitoju.

3. Build confidence to progress. Make sure you are showcasing wherever possible successful people from minority groups in the way in which you use examples when you are talking, so that you are inspiring them all the time. One way of doing this is by actively sponsoring people from under-represented groups and champion them for promotion. While mentoring is important, it assumes that they need help to develop and build confidence, according to Otitoju, while sponsorship says "I'm going go fly your flag and wear your T shirt".

WHAT TO DO NEXT

- Reflect on the benefits of having a diverse team for innovation, performance and understanding of your clients, as digital innovation is normally made for a large and broad audience.

- Employ measures to work with and attract a diverse team.

- Periodically review your diversity measures to check progress and stay current with what is happening in the world.

FURTHER READING

Making your Voice Heard by Connson Chou Locke

Diversity Inc: the Failed Promise of a Billion-Dollar Business by Pamela Newkirk

Hearts and minds: Harnessing leadership, culture, and talent to really go digital by Lucy Kung (free to download)

CHAPTER 7

SUDDEN IMPACT: BLACK SWANS AND COCKROACH UNICORNS

B y drawing together what you have learnt from this book, and taking steps to future-proof yourself, you can be prepared for whatever transformation comes your way during your career, spotting opportunities for you, your team or company. This will help you to deal with disruption that, according to an EY report on megatrends, "comes from far afield. It can emerge from uncontrollable wildfires, geopolitical power shifts or a global pandemic that shuts down society and commerce".

Not only that, automation, in tandem with a Covid-related recession, is creating a double-disruption scenario for workers, the World Economic Forum (WEF) report on the future of work says.

These types of events are black swans – those rare occurrences that have a widespread impact, such as the global financial crisis in 2008. They could even be the precursor to a larger uncertainty – climate change.

The year 2020 was dismal for many companies, but some shone and proved to be crisis-resistant, such as pharmaceutical groups developing vaccines, retailers offering goods online and tech groups riding the wave of remote working.

They demonstrated survival skills akin to cockroaches, which are reportedly one of the few insects able to survive a nuclear war. Putting the term together with unicorns, which are fast-growing start-ups valued at more than $1 billion, you have a 'cockroach unicorn' which is a resilient company that can adapt to uncertainty rapidly.

Those companies, and their employees, were able to capitalise on opportunities and act fast towards a digital future in an unpredictable world.

LESSONS LEARNT

Deloitte looked at how businesses were coping with the unexpected challenges of the pandemic.

Businesses that bounced back from unpredictability typically shared similar traits: they had been prepared, they adapted and were flexible, they collaborated and they had high levels of trust and responsibility.

In order for you to successfully navigate change, we believe you can draw on these traits to use personally by mixing them with the themes we have explored throughout this book.

TACTIC 1: PREPARE

As we saw in Chapter 1, planning is key to navigating transformation and being prepared for what comes your way. While your plans may not be for any specific black swan event, they can help to broaden the options available to you should the unexpected happen. The more prepared for change you are, the more resilient you can be in the face of the obstacles to overcome and the more positive your mindset will be to get you through the challenges.

The most successful companies planned for eventualities and acted early. "Resilient organisations should prepare playbooks that anticipate potential events", the Deloitte report says.

Resilience was also identified by the WEF as one of the top ten skills needed in 2025.

As managers, you are the ones who will be at the coalface: planning, managing and executing change.

The disruption caused by the pandemic has shown us the "importance of planning for the unknown", according to the Work 2035 report by Citrix on how people and technology will pioneer new ways of working. "It is no longer a question of how or when the employee experience will change since it already has . . . but we need to understand, this is only the beginning", it says.

"Be prepared for everything", says Elisabetta Galli, a former senior executive at Spanish bank Santander. "The reality is that something negative always occurs, and if you are prepared up front, you will be able to manage that."

And Kanwarjit Singh, a senior executive in the health sector, agrees: "You have to be ready and prepared for radical transformation . . . and it can be something that moves very quickly."

IN SUMMARY

- By being prepared you are more able to deal with the unexpected.
- Planning for change can build resilience.
- Keep an eye on trends in your sector to help you plan ahead.

EXERCISE

By using EY's 'Megatrends and future-back' strategy, you can expose your team to trends usually outside the scope of their focus, thereby reducing the risk of "missing the next big thing". The report mentions four primary forces that will shape the future:

- *Powering human augmentation: technology*
- *Beyond globalisation*
- *Gen Z rising: demographics*
- *Exponential climate impact: environment*

You can use the megatrends to envisage multiple future scenarios, customising the list to suit your line of business.

Take each one and spend time to think about and note how these forces will affect your organisation and sector. Research papers, reports and articles from reputable sources to build up your knowledge of trends.

You can also brainstorm these points with your team as a creative and useful exercise to strengthen bonds and motivation as they feel more involved in planning processes.

TACTIC 2: ADAPT, FLEX AND FAIL FAST

All of the companies we spoke to were using some form of agile working practices, where multi-disciplinary teams were collaborating and taking an iterative approach to develop new products for their consumers.

Having a workforce that was adaptable and flexible was key and Deloitte's report also identified these as the most crucial traits to a company's futures. 54 per cent of chief executives selected it as one of the top three most critical traits.

Dynamic teams can speed up decision-making and increase innovation while siloed departments can be slower to react to change.

Global bank BBVA had taken the decentralised approach one radical step further by setting up so-called 'liquid pools' where permanent staff operate in an internal market and are temporarily assigned to work on transformation projects.

This helps to break down silos or structures in an organisation, as well as changing the linear managerial relationships, making teams more agile and better equipped to respond to changing business needs.

In certain disciplines, such as design, behavioural economics or data, most positions are no longer 'resources' that belong to a specific department. Instead, they respond to project objectives, says Marta Javaloys, change agent leading transformation at the Spanish bank BBVA.

Collaboration externally, within and beyond industries, is also vital so that organisations do not tackle "big disruptions alone", the Deloitte report says. This was a view reflected in some of the companies we spoke to, which we covered in Chapter 3, where innovation hubs had been set up to help build an intrapreneurial culture within organisations.

While they spoke of having a culture of so-called failure, what this really meant in practice was experimentation that did not hit the bottom line. When projects did fail, it was essential that lessons were learnt so that any benefits or insights could be used to build back better in the future.

As Meri Williams, former Chief Technology Officer at challenger bank Monzo, puts it: "The art of management is to make it safe enough to learn through minor failure without letting someone go so far out on a limb that the major failure tanks the company, person's career or the team. That tension is quite tough."

IN SUMMARY

- Get your project off the ground quickly.
- Review, assess and pivot if necessary.
- Close it down quickly if it is not meeting milestones.

TACTIC 3: BUILD TRUST

Trust is key to communication and transparency across the workforce and successful managers lead with empathy.

The Deloitte report found that more than a third of responding chief executives were not confident their organisations had done enough to develop trust between leaders and employees. Those who were succeeding, though, focused on improving communication and transparency with key stakeholders.

It is paramount to maintain or develop trust within your teams, which we covered in Chapter 4. The key point is as a manager you will need to be able to connect, understand, motivate and listen as well as be authentic for your team to feel you are being honest.

The questions that pop up frequently with millennials are "What do you stand for? And can I trust you?" says Gerd Leonhard, a European-based futurist who looks at business trends over the next three to five years.

Authenticity, empathy and logic are also pivotal in effective communication to deliver successful transformation projects because they are the foundations of building trust.

All of these help to build a shared vision of what it is going to take to make change happen and you will also be able to influence and persuade colleagues to buy into it, because you are trustworthy.

"You need to convince and influence to make clear to everyone that transformation is good and everybody has a part to play in it", says Galli.

IN SUMMARY

■ Trustworthiness is vital. Maintain and develop trust.

■ Be transparent and communicate more effectively and often.

■ You will then be able to influence and persuade colleagues to buy into a shared vision.

WHERE SUSTAINABILITY, VALUES AND TECH MEET

Environmental sustainability is a huge trend as concerns over climate change drive consumers to look for products and brands that align with their personal values, which in turn has an impact on company strategy.

People "expect institutions to align their actions to a higher or meaningful purpose and put the needs of their customers, employees, contractors, communities, and the planet at the forefront", Deloitte's report says.

From banking and insurance to retailers and fashion groups, companies are keen to present themselves as being pro the planet while not becoming entangled in 'greenwashing' claims, where organisations, such as oil groups, are accused of deceptively presenting themselves as environmentally friendly.

Connie Nam, founder of online jeweller Astrid & Miyu, agrees: "I'm mindful of companies greenwashing and just paying for it to neutralise carbon footprint."

She was reviewing every stage in the supply chain with a view to making improvements. She was aiming to use 100 per cent recycled material for packaging, for example (see box on page 126). "We have a no packet, no packaging option as well with customers, which a lot of customers actually opted in for", she says.

Among other companies we spoke to, Mapfre and Santander had worked to change their image among Generation Z (those born from 1996 to 2010) and millennials (those born from 1981 to 1996). The Gen Z cohort is particularly important because people aged between ten and 24 total 1.8 billion, making up 24 per cent of the global population, according to EY analysis. They are the workers and consumers of the future.

"Customer acquisition or retention is going to be harder now if we do not understand our role in this society, and the value we can bring to people", says Pablo Fernandez Iglesias, Head of Business Development and Innovation at insurer Mapfre Assistance. "Insurance brings peace of mind and security to society. So we need to improve our understanding of this new reality, based on ecosystems and interaction with others. And on top of that, we cannot forget that we live in a world that needs to be more sustainable so this needs to be part of our business model. It is no longer a game of making profit for the investors only. We cannot forget the world in which we are living in order to make business."

Elisabetta Galli, a former Santander executive, agrees: "Sustainability values are very important and being able to interlock these elements that are cultural with the technology is a key success factor for any company."

Santander carried out research and held interviews with digital talent the bank targeted in the marketplace.

"The first question we asked was, would you work for a bank? And the typical answer was: 'Are you kidding me? I would prefer to go to the dentist.' These were typical answers because they have an image of the bank as evil. So this is really something we have to fight against and to project a different image."

Demonstrating you are committed to sustainability, protecting the environment and supporting people's needs, helping them to achieve their goals can help you and your business to prosper. "This can make a difference in the perception that people have, and in the attraction of talent", says Galli.

To succeed at managing this situation in the workplace, you will have to be able to puzzle together an instant picture of many complex issues at the same time, including making sure your teams are diverse where everyone's voice is heard.

"Purpose includes values, ethics, and understanding what you stand for, and sustainability is a big part of this", says Gerd Leonhard, a futurist.

You need to be aware of trends in technology that are likely to help us to work better and smarter whether it is using data to predict consumer behaviour, blockchain for smart contracts or automated chat bots.

One of the main reasons we 'go digital' is to find faster and more resource-efficient ways to operate and reach our audiences and scale up fast.

IN SUMMARY

- Interlock sustainability, values and tech in what you do.
- Demonstrate the positive impact your work has.
- Understand what you stand for.

CONNIE NAM

Founder of Astrid & Miyu, UK-based jeweller

Connie Nam is keen to reduce the carbon footprint of her online jewellery business because it not only makes environmental sense but commercial sense as well. She has reviewed every stage in the supply chain with a view to making improvements and is aiming to use 100 per cent recycled material for packaging. "We have a no packet, no packaging option as well with customers, which a lot of customers actually opted in for", she says.

"We can't claim that we're fully sustainable yet. But we're definitely making small steps to do the right thing and have very tangible plans in place. The last thing I want to do is simply pay to neutralise carbon footprint", she says.

In 2020 Astrid & Miyu started prototyping all its product samples through 3D printing locally because the pandemic disrupted supply chains. Before then, it had used a mix of 3D printing and sending designs to Asia and then waiting four to eight weeks for the turnaround. But that was no longer a wait it could afford. "We just started doing more 3D printing, because we were desperate. And we thought, why didn't we do this before?"

Not only did this reduce the company's carbon footprint, but it also cut lead times by four weeks. It was so successful that the company was in the process of acquiring 3D printing in-house.

Astrid & Miyu will still continue full production in Asia, but Nam will also be looking at European production to reduce the carbon footprint further.

CHANGING WAYS OF WORKING

By 2025, the time spent on current tasks at work by humans and machines will be equal, the World Economic Forum's (WEF) report on the future of work says.

The WEF estimates that by 2025, 85 million jobs may be displaced by a shift in the division of labour between humans and machines, while 97 million new roles may emerge that are more adapted to the new division of labour between humans, machines and algorithms.

Automation of processes and the streamlining of businesses will have an impact on the way people work where they will still do tasks that are difficult for machines. This will include work that needs to use intuition, imagination and "true understanding, instant for a human to understand another human", says Gerd Leonhard, a futurist.

In Citrix's Work 2035 report, most of the respondents believed that in 2028 businesses would be earning more money from AI or from data orientation rather than from their human counterparts.

"It doesn't mean people go away", says Michelle Senecal de Fonseca, a senior executive at Citrix. "After Covid, people realised that the importance of human beings is actually higher than they had thought about it a few years before.

"How do you have an argument with an algorithm? How do you explain something? There has to be an escalation path. Or how do you feel engaged if all you get is work from an AI bot?" says Senecal de Fonseca about the future of work, with a piece of software replacing managers. "It's not an algorithm that you work for, you work for people with purposes."

THE KEY TO REMOTE WORKING

The flexibility of remote working is here to stay for many white-collar workers, with companies adopting a hybrid pattern when office life resumes, whether that is working a couple of days a week from home or mostly remotely.

84 per cent of employers are set to rapidly digitalise working processes, including a significant expansion of remote work, with the potential to move 44 per cent of their workforce to operate remotely, the World Economic Forum report on the future of work says.

The key to remote working is seeing it as 'distributed working' – you are not working independently but as part of a team or network with other colleagues online.

To succeed at this, it is likely to require a shift in mindset. Part of that means we have to understand when people prefer to work and how, trust them to do it and work to objectives. To address concerns about productivity and well-being, about one-third of all employers expect to take steps to create a sense of community, connection and belonging among employees through digital tools, and to tackle the well-being challenges posed by the shift to remote work, the WEF report says.

It means that we have to work in a network harmoniously and respectful of individual workers' needs and preferences. In this way, we can increase performance and create a culture that attracts the best talent whether they are near or far.

Not only are workers demanding the flexibility but there are strong commercial reasons too, with potential rental and travel savings for businesses, helping them to reduce their carbon footprint.

Hogan Lovells, for example, was due to cut back on travel and not have so many management face-to-face meetings. "Partner events will happen much more infrequently", says Michael Davison, Deputy Chief Executive of the law firm.

"Lots of employers have found working remotely very doable and very efficient", says Anne Boden, founder of Starling bank. She was not intending to expand her business's commercial space and was due to consider hybrid working patterns of days at home and in the office.

Citrix took it a step further and announced that its workers can decide where they want to work from 2021. "If you're hired in the UK but you really want to live in your second home in the country or go back home to Spain but work somewhere else, we are going to permit it", says Senecal de Fonseca.

"There are lots of things we have to think about so this is a work in progress, taxation, time, your vacation, pay packages, how close you need to be to a centre, how often you would be expected to come in. We have got a lot to learn but I think that is a really bold step from our corporate leadership."

While this may work for workers who have separate rooms for studies, it was hard for employees who were working in their bedroom or felt isolated. Some people are going to find the isolation and the workspace "difficult", says Boden.

It also brought challenges as managing people via video-conferencing requires different skills. Colleagues had to be trusted to be responsible and carry out their tasks. Communication had to go into super-drive.

Previously, when you had a face-to-face meeting and you would wait for the most senior person's agenda to open before talking, or if people were required to travel, the number of people attending would be limited because of the expense. "That doesn't happen any more", says Senecal de Fonseca at Citrix. "You can get people a little bit faster. You can have a wider array of people. Probably more integration of teams, as more departments come together and you can have more frequent conversations."

"A lot of it is shifting your ability to be a manager", she says, because using video conferencing technology such as Zoom or Microsoft Teams "democratises an organisation". "Everybody is pretty much equal on a Zoom screen", she says.

It also raised retention questions, such as:

- How do you onboard new recruits when most people are working remotely?
- How do you build new relationships and make professional connections?
- How do you ensure you are visible with senior managers in order to gain promotion?

One trainee told Michael Davison at Hogan Lovells that the experience of a six-month rotation in his department was "ok but they didn't know what the department was like. They said they didn't feel they made connections".

And over time, the lack of making connections can affect your advancement. One study by Nicholas Bloom, a professor of economics at Stanford University, found that people who worked from home after 21 months had almost half the promotion rate of people that are in the office, despite performing better than their colleagues in the office.

Over time this is likely to become problematic, especially with diversity initiatives. "Five to ten years from now, you'll have a much higher promotion rate of single young men than married women with young kids. And for any other trait where people are split down on preferences, the people living far away from the office won't get promoted", he told the website Reset Work.

But many companies intend to keep some commercial space but perhaps just not expand further. "We are not getting rid of buildings because we will always need that for learning", says Senecal de Fonseca. "You can't stop the personal interaction. That's really why people work."

WHAT DO YOU NEED TO DO TO BE AHEAD OF THE CURVE?

Most people have to modernise to stay relevant professionally, keeping up to date with the latest code, frameworks and ways of working as industries are changing rapidly.

In the next ten years, we are going to see rapid advances, such as language recognition, in intelligent assistance and simple, routine tasks, including financial transactions, advice and investing. Even driving is likely to be carried out by machines.

As automation displaces jobs, the question will be whether new roles can be developed fast enough to absorb those who are displaced and can organisations upskill the people to be able to make that shift.

The employees who succeed in this environment will be largely those that have a growth mindset and have emotional intelligence, which we explored in Chapter 4, where they are constantly learning, keeping an eye on what is changing and being selective about what to be involved with.

The World Economic Forum listed the top skills for 2025 in its Future of Jobs report. They include:

- analytical and critical thinking
- active learning
- complex problem-solving
- creativity and originality
- resilience and emotional intelligence.

These are the skills you should focus on and nurture for you and the talent you will need to keep on adding value and to stay ahead of the curve. Being able to keep learning is a key aptitude that the companies we spoke to look for when hiring. Mindset can be more important than skill set.

"Nurturing a genuine learning attitude is the answer", says Elisabetta Galli, former Global Head of Knowledge, Development and Talent Management at the Spanish bank Santander. "It's important to challenge yourself, to put yourself in the first line to experiment to learn a new methodology to use new tools", she says.

The tech and telecoms industry has always competed for new skills, new types of coding or new backgrounds, where a limited number of people who have the skills were poached by rival companies.

But "you can't do that any more because IT and telecoms companies are not the only ones using this skill base", says Senecal de Fonseca.

"They are needed in absolutely every industry and therefore we have to broaden the pool. Every company is going to have to take the talent they have already got and upskill them along with having a social responsibility of bringing new ones into your organisation and training them."

These types of workers in demand are also data literate. The use of data, which we explored in Chapter 5, whether at individual or team level, will only grow and inform your decisions.

Successful people also usually develop mastery by making choices of what to focus on. "They don't try to learn all the new things all the time and focus on every new trend", says Meri Williams, former Chief Technology Officer at challenger bank Monzo. But they do "maximise the opportunity to transfer skills. To see how something that they learnt before could be reusable".

This is endorsed by what companies look for when they hire people. "The people who are excited by change are the kind of people you want to recruit in a business", says Michael Davison at Hogan Lovells.

You also have to be even more open to change and adapting to accelerating trends.

"It's not a choice any more", says Tom Fortin, former Managing Director of BlackRock. "It's now life or death."

And one trap to avoid is to keep doing the same type of job repetitively for years without really learning any new skills or stretching yourself.

"Do you have ten years' experience or one year of experience teb times? And you can get one year of experience ten times just by doing the same job the same old way in a few different settings", says Williams.

Having said that, another theme in transformation is that you should not be afraid of making your role redundant or of replacing yourself.

"People who replace themselves always find another bigger, better thing to do. This is career advancement", says Anastasia Leng, co-founder of start-up CreativeX. "The whole concept of digital transformation can be very scary for some people because it means there are certain things technology is going to do . . . or another party is going to do it. If you can bring digital transformation into your company and execute it successfully you are very much on the fast track to promotion and growth rather than out the door."

And if you are feeling especially bold after working for several years in the same organisation, take a year off to reset your mind. This is the advice from Alberto Levy, international MBA professor and start-up mentor at IE Business School in Madrid. His personal statement is "to be disruptive" with your thoughts.

His point is that after you have been in a role for several years, you stop seeing things and you can lose perspective. If you can take a break to do something different you will benefit the next organisation you work for, bringing a fresh perspective.

You may be able to explore what the options are around this if you cannot afford to take a year off. Sabbaticals, unpaid leave and flexible working are all other practical ways to take a reset if they are on offer in your company. It will give you time to think and even play.

Nneile Nkholise, founder 3D-IMO, a South African start-up, believes in "embracing the beauty of play" by spending a day with toddlers to reset creativity in order to understand digital transformation. "They don't care about failure. They don't care about trying out new things. They will do everything as crazy and messed up as it is until they get something really right. So you need to step into the shoes of a young child and get messy because the backbone of transformation is creativity and innovation."

IN SUMMARY

- Develop mastery by choosing what to focus on.
- Be open to constantly learning.
- Take time out to think to boost creativity.

WE WANT TO HEAR FROM YOU

We would like to hear from you about how you are making digital transformation happen in your workplace. We would like you to share your experiences, the good, the bad, the unexpected for our ongoing research. Please join the conversation on our LinkedIn group: Going Digital: what it takes for smoother transformations.

Here are some specific questions to start the conversation:

- Do you have any positive advice on what steps you have taken to deliver digital transformation?
- What challenges have you encountered?
- And how did you deal with them?

Contact us directly at:

Lyndsey Jones, LinkedIn profile: www.linkedin.com/in/lyndsey-jones/-389b6830/

Twitter: @LyndseyJones129

Balvinder Singh Powar, LinkedIn profile: www.linkedin.com/in/balvindersinghpowar/

Twitter: @balpowar

We may use what you tell us in future writing but we would disguise the source. We may or may not be able to answer you but we really do want to hear from you.

FURTHER READING

No Rules Rules: Netflix and the Culture of Reinvention by Reed Hastings and Erin Meyer

Our Iceberg is Melting by John Kotter

Imagine It Forward: Courage, Creativity, and the Power of Change by Beth Comstock

Mindset: Changing the way you think to fulfil your potential by Carol Dweck

REFERENCES

Chapter 1

McKinsey report 2020:

How COVID-19 has pushed companies over the technology tipping point–and transformed business forever

FT news stories:

'Prospering in the pandemic: the top 100 companies'

'Do young people really need the office?'

'How to avoid the return of office cliques'

Adam Kreek:

CLEAR goals are better than SMART goals

Deloitte UK report:

Capturing the digital opportunity for British Sport

'Who is Alexander Osterwalder?' by Daniel Periera, 6 January 2021

Business Model Generation: A Handbook for Visionaries, Game Changers, and Challengers (The Strategyzer series) by Alexander Osterwalder

Prosci:

Primary sponsor's role and importance

Chapter 2

'Choosing Strategies for Change' by John Kotter and Leonard Schlesinger in *Harvard Business Review Magazine,* March–April 1979

'Six change approaches' by Kotter & Schlesinger on Expert Program Management

'Resistance to change: three models to overcome it' by Lorenzo Federico Sacerdote

Simon Sinek TED talk: 'How great leaders inspire action'

Banking on it: How I Disrupted an Industry by Anne Boden (pp 119, 120, 126)

FT news stories:

'Mizuho chief predicts wave of Covid M&A and succession shake-ups'

'Bank Possible's future in question as Starling team flies apart'

Chapter 3

'Britain's best will embrace change and thrive again,' by Amanda Murphy in *The Sunday Times Top Track 100 Covid-19 edition,* 5 July 2020

Banking on it: How I Disrupted an Industry by Anne Boden (p 249)

www.kaizen.com/what-is-kaizen.html

www.toyota-europe.com/world-of-toyota/this-is-toyota/the-toyota-way

'Zara Owner's Lean Business Model Helps It Cope With Pandemic' by Rodrigo Orihuela in *Bloomberg Technology,* 16 September 2020

The Lean Start-up by Eric Ries (p 8)

www.lean.org/whatslean/

Agile Manifesto: https://agilemanifesto.org/

What is Agile?: www.atlassian.com/agile; www.visual-paradigm.com/scrum/scrum-vs-waterfall-vs-agile-vs-lean-vs-kanban/

'Lean management or agile? The right answer may be both', McKinsey article, 14 July 2020

Peter Drucker quote:

'Large organizations cannot be versatile. A large organization is effective through its mass rather than through its agility. Fleas can jump many times their own height, but not an elephant.'

Robin Kwong:

https://robinkwong.com/cnl/

'The Effect of Organizational Structure on Open Innovation' by Junyeong Lee, Jinyoung Min and Heeseok Lee in *ScienceDirect,* Vol 91, 2016 (pp 492–501)

FT news stories:

'Microsoft growth accelerates as pandemic boosts cloud business'

'Cloud business reaps rewards of the work-from-home revolution'

McKinsey Global Survey report, 5 October 2020:

How COVID-19 has pushed companies over the technology tipping point—and transformed business forever

Smarter with Gartner:

Gartner Top Strategic Technology Trends for 2021

5 Habits of Organizations With Successful Artificial Intelligence (AI) Projects

KPMG report:

Expect the Unexpected: Building business value in a changing world

Chapter 4

Working with emotional Intelligence by Daniel Goleman

Drive: The surprising truth about what motivates us by Daniel H Pink

2020 Edelman Trust Barometer

'Begin with Trust' by Frances X. Frei and Anne Morriss in *Harvard Business Review*, May–June 2020

An interview with Meredith Belbin:

www.youtube.com/watch?v=XPMN9N6NC7k

Belbin team roles:

www.belbin.com/about/belbin-team-roles

'Belbin Team Role Theories' by Peter Mackechnie (www.BusinessCoaching.co.uk)

'AI on the Horizon by Headspring':

https://go.headspringexecutive.com/AIReport

Comparably:

'Happiest employees 2020'

FT news story:

Zoom's sales surge beats even most optimistic forecasts

'It's time to end the workplace taboo around mental health' by Antonio Horta-Osorio in *The Guardian*, 1 May 2018

Deloitte report:

Mental health and employers: refreshing the case for investment

Chapter 5

US Chamber of Commerce Foundation:

Big Data and What it Means

seotribunal.com:

63 Fascinating Google Search Statistics

Domo:

Business Intelligence Resources

McKinsey report:

Achieving business impact with data

PwC:

Build your data foundation

'Former subpostmasters expected to have names cleared after court
appeal', *The Guardian,* 24 April 2021

Information Commissioner's Office (ICO):

Right to restrict processing

General Data Protection Regulation (GDPR) Compliance Guidelines

Federal Trade Commission tips and advice:

Privacy and Security

Lexology:

Overview of data protection laws in Africa

Deloitte Global Data Maturity report:

Digital transformation through data

'How managers should use data', video with Professor Thomas H
Davenport

FT news story:

'WhatsApp delays privacy changes that led to user outcry'

Questions on what to do next took inspiration from this article on devising
and implementing a successful data strategy:

'How to Create a Data Strategy: 7 Things Every Business Must Include'
by Bernard Marr, Forbes.com

Chapter 6

Global Diversity Practice:

What is Diversity & Inclusion?

McKinsey report:

Delivering growth through diversity in the workplace

'The Other Diversity Dividend' by Paul Gompers and Silpa Kovvali,
Harvard Business Review, July–August 2018

FT news story:

'Five steps on the path to digital transformation'

Digital Trends story:

Skin Tone, Heart Rate Sensors, and a Push for Accuracy

NBC news:

Apple Confirms #TattooGate Problem is Real

Sunday Times story:

'Racist' self-driving cars may not spot dark faces

Guardian story:

'Skin in the frame: black photographers welcome Google initiative'

Law Commission report:

Automated Vehicles: Summary of Consultation Paper 3 – A regulatory framework for automated vehicles, p 12, Equity note 2.57

Acas:

Dealing with unconscious bias: Improving equality, diversity and inclusion in your workplace

FT news story:

'KPMG appoints first female leaders in shake-up after Michael furore'

The Greater La Crosse Area Diversity Council:

Harvard Implicit Association Test

'Gender differences in speed of advancement: An empirical examination of top executives in the Fortune 100 firms' by Bonet in *Strategic Management Journal*, 6 January 2020 (Wiley Online Library)

'6 ways to improve diversity in your workplace' by Sophia Lee in *Torch,* 8 March 2021

'Is unconscious bias training still worthwhile?' by Frederick Herbert in *LSE Business Review,* 24 Arch 2021

Chapter 7

Ey-megatrends-2020-report: pp 4,16

World Economic Forum report:

The Future_of_Jobs_2020, pp 5, 29, 36

Digital News Project 2021:

Journalism, Media and Technology Trends and Predictions 2021, p 35

Citrix report:

Work 2035: How people and technology will pioneer new ways of working

Deloitte insights:

Five characteristics of resilient organizations

Insider Reviews:

Sustainability sells: Why consumers and clothing brands alike are turning to sustainability as a guiding light

Deloitte Insights:

Building the Resilient Organisation

Digital News Project 2021:

Journalism, Media and Technology Trends and Predictions 2021

Nicholas Bloom interview:

'What research says about how to make hybrid work succeed'

www.unfoldwork.com – a company helping with mindset, skill set and tool sets to make deep work happen via distributed working

INDEX